The Jesus Prayer

The Jesus Prayer

THE ANCIENT DESERT PRAYER
THAT TUNES THE HEART TO GOD

Frederica Mathewes-Green

PARACLETE PRESS
BREWSTER, MASSACHUSETTS

The Jesus Prayer: The Ancient Desert Prayer That Tunes the Heart to God

2010 Second Priting
2009 First Printing

Copyright © 2009 by Frederica Mathewes-Green

ISBN 978-1-55725-659-1

Unless otherwise indicated, all Scripture quotations are taken from the Revised Standard Version of the Bible, copyright © 1952 [2nd edition, 1971] by the Division of Christian Education of the National Council of the Churches of Christ in the United States of America. Used by permission. All rights reserved.

Library of Congress Cataloging-in-Publication Data

Mathewes-Green, Frederica.
  The Jesus prayer : the ancient desert prayer that tunes the heart to God / Frederica Mathewes-Green.
      p. cm.
  Includes bibliographical references.
  ISBN 978-1-55725-659-1
  1. Jesus prayer. I. Title.
  BT590.J28M38 2009
  242'.72--dc22

                              2009025235

10 9 8 7 6 5 4 3 2

Published by Paraclete Press
Brewster, Massachusetts
www.paracletepress.com
Printed in the United States of America

Contents

Introduction

I t was about 2:30 in the morning when I got out of bed last night to pray. I have been doing this since I was pregnant with my first baby, decades ago; I had read somewhere that the middle of the night was a good time to have your daily prayers, with silence before and silence afterward, and no phones to ring. I thought it sounded like a good habit to establish, since I'd be getting up with the baby anyway.

Over the years there were three babies, and eventually three teenagers, and now three young-marrieds with babies of their own. Now the household is down to my husband and me again. All these years I've been getting up in the night to pray. It's a necessity now, and I need it like I need food and light.

About fifteen years ago I started to use the Jesus Prayer during these mid-night hours: "Lord Jesus Christ, Son of God, have mercy on me." This very simple prayer was developed in the deserts of Egypt and Palestine during the early centuries of Christian faith, and has been practiced in the Eastern Orthodox Church ever since. It is a prayer inspired by St. Paul's exhortation to "pray constantly" (1 Thess. 5:17), and its purpose is to tune one's inner attention to the presence of the Lord.

But what is that nameless thing, the "inner attention"? When we talk about feeling God's presence, we're accustomed to speak as if such experiences arose from our emotions. Yet when I had my rather dramatic conversion experience, decades ago, it sure seemed more objective than that. At the time, the best way I could describe it was to say that "a little radio switched on inside me," and I became aware of Christ speaking to me. (It wasn't something I heard with my ears, but by an inner voice, filling my awareness.)

I never knew what to make of that "little radio"; it didn't fit our familiar division of people into "head" and "heart." But as I began to read the literature of Eastern Christianity, I found that they were familiar with this "little radio." They even had a word for it: the *nous*. It's a word that recurs through the Greek New Testament, but we don't have a good equivalent in English. It gets translated "mind," but it doesn't mean the talkative mind, the one that cogitates and constructs theories. It is a receptive capacity of the intellect; we could call it "the understanding" or "the comprehension." The Eastern Church has always known that the nous can be trained to register, or perceive, the voice of God.

That is where the Jesus Prayer comes in. The idea is to spend some time every day practicing the Prayer. You pray it fifty or a hundred times, or more, or less; not robotically but sincerely, speaking to Christ while pulling together your attention to the best of your ability. You get the Prayer going other times, too, whenever you think of it, while waiting at a stoplight or brushing your teeth. This brief, all-purpose, very portable prayer takes root and spreads.

In the process, you hone your ability to discern God's presence. He is already there, of course; we just aren't very good at perceiving it. Practicing the Jesus Prayer helps you sharpen your ability to "tune in" to his presence, just as you would practice scales to hone your ability to identify musical pitch.

So last night I awoke, as usual, without an alarm—sometime in the middle of the night I just swim up to consciousness. I went out into the hallway and stood on the worn spot in the carpet, in front of the bookcase, and looked up at the icon of Christ. A blue light was slanting in the window from my study, filtering between the large, heart-shaped leaves of the catalpa tree. Our street, a simple curve on a hilltop, was still. Sometimes, if I wake up later, I hear an early-rising robin robustly anticipating the dawn (and probably annoying all the other birds, who are still trying to get some shut-eye), but last night it was too early even for him.

I looked into the face of Christ, illuminated softly now by candlelight. I made the sign of the cross. I said some preliminary prayers, including the Lord's Prayer and the Nicene Creed, and recited Psalm 51, the prayer that David offered when he repented for seducing Bathsheba and murdering her husband. I've heard that you should "warm up your heart" before beginning the Jesus Prayer, and these preliminaries help do that; the Creed reminds me of the majesty of God, while Psalm 51 reminds me of my neediness, my damaged, greedy condition.

After that, I began repeating the Jesus Prayer in my mind, over and over, in an unhurried way: "Lord Jesus Christ, have mercy on me." (The words can be varied a bit; I use a shorter version, while the standard form is, "Lord Jesus Christ, Son of God, have mercy on me." My husband uses an even longer version, praying, "Lord Jesus Christ, Son of the Living God, have mercy on me, a sinner," the last phrase an echo of the tax collector's prayer in Jesus' parable.) I aim to say this prayer a hundred times, and keep track by moving my fingers along a prayer rope, a loop of silken cord tied with a hundred elaborate knots. When my mind wanders—which it does, believe me, over and over every night—I back up a few knots and focus in again.

This practice of saying the Jesus Prayer is accurately termed a spiritual discipline; it's a disciplined learning process, like learning to play the cello. It takes perseverance and focused attention. For a cellist, the tedium of practicing scales must appear so distant from the final goal, when that beautiful, dark music will spill forth fluidly. Yet, one day, the cellist will pick up her bow, and she and the instrument will have become one.

So I keep on asking Christ for mercy, working the Prayer deep into my awareness. I say it a hundred times at night, and throughout the day I set it going in my mind as often as I remember (hopefully, at least once an hour). But it is the focused mid-night prayer time that really enables it to root down deep.

And gradually I am coming to see that it is true. It really is possible to sense the presence of God—continuously.

I hasten to add that I *don't* sense it continuously. To be completely honest, I don't want to. I'd rather slide away into thinking about things that attract me, or anger me, or frighten me, and behave as if I can deal with them on my own. Apparently I think I can pull down a window shade between God and me, and do things the way I want to without him finding out.

That's ridiculous, of course; if I turned my back on him and ran away as fast as I could, wherever I stopped he would have beaten me there. "Whither shall I go from thy Spirit? Or whither shall I flee from thy presence? If I ascend to heaven, thou art there! If I make my bed in Sheol, thou art there!" (Ps. 139:7–8).

But he is loving and very patient, and when I'm ready to turn and look at him again, I find that he has been continuing all that time to hold me in his steady gaze. Then the Prayer rises up inside, and makes a connection like a lamp plugging into a socket.

This prayer is not designed to generate fancy mystical experiences or soppy emotions. Yet it works away steadily inside, gradually building a sure connection with the Lord. Where the Lord enters in, there is light; I can see many ways that he has changed me over the years, illuminating and dispelling reflexive lying thoughts and fears. My part was just to keep showing up, day after day, for these quiet sessions with him.

The Prayer's goal is to help you keep always in touch with the presence of God. Some of you are already saying, "This is for me. This is what I've always wanted." You know what I mean by "the presence of God," because you've felt it yourself. And whether it was on one or two memorable occasions, or regularly over the years, you agree that it is intoxicating. When I try to describe it, I find I use the word *beauty* more often than any other. You know what I'm talking about, and you're eager to hear more.

But some of you feel sad when you hear people talk of such experiences. You've never felt anything you would describe as "the presence of God." You wonder why you've been left out. Has God rejected you?

The first thing I want to tell you is this: the very fact that you want to know God's presence means you're already sensing *something*. Think about it. How many people never give God a second thought? How many people sleep in on Sunday morning, and never open a Bible or send up a prayer? But you're not like that; you really want to be closer to the Lord. My hunch is that you are already sensing something of God's presence, or you wouldn't care.

Here's a homely analogy: picture yourself walking around a shopping mall, looking at the people and the window displays. Suddenly, you get a whiff of cinnamon. You weren't even hungry, but now you really crave a cinnamon roll. This craving isn't something you made up. There you were, minding your own business, when some drifting molecules of sugar, butter, and spice collided with a susceptible patch inside your nose. You had a real encounter with cinnamon— not a mental delusion, not an emotional projection, but the real thing.

And what was the effect? You want more, *now*. And if you hunger to know the presence of God, it's because, I believe, you have already begun to scent its compelling delight.

So, if you're one of those people who think that you've never had an experience of God, ask yourself: Why do you even care? Why do you spend time praying? Why do you bother to read the Bible, or books about prayer? The world is full of ways to waste your time. But if you picture yourself giving up on prayer, you feel hollow, desolated. All this must be doing *something*, even if you can't put your finger on it.

The Prayer can help you learn to perceive that something, and do so more consistently and accurately.

About now some of you are thinking, "Well, I certainly have wandered into the wrong room." You don't recognize yourself here at all. You're not much for churchgoing. You're not even sure you would call yourself a Christian. But you do want to grow spiritually, and you want to know God better. Is it all right for you to use the Prayer too?

As we'll see, in the Christian East, homeland of the Jesus Prayer, there is some opinion that it can be harmful to practice the Jesus Prayer if you are not fully engaged in the life of the Orthodox Church, receiving the sacraments and guided by a wise spiritual elder. So, if some think it's unwise even for non-Orthodox Christians to take up the Prayer, then it would certainly be too risky for a non-Christian to attempt it.

I don't expect those concerns will dissuade such readers who still want to try it, however. So I'll just give a word of advice. The spiritual realm is real, I have found, and not all the forces in it are benign. The less benign powers are associated, in particular, with lying (Jn. 8:44). This is a context, then, in which it is not wise to practice insincerity or hypocrisy. Perhaps you admire Jesus of Nazareth as an important historical figure and an eloquent teacher—but the Prayer commits you to more than that. The first word of the Prayer is *Lord*, a statement that you acknowledge Jesus of Nazareth as your Lord. Then you call him "Christ," from the Greek word meaning "Anointed One," or, in Hebrew, "the Messiah."

Those are some significant assertions, and if you don't agree with them, ask yourself why you *want* to pray the Prayer. You may feel that, for reasons you can't identify, it just seems to be calling to you. That is an interesting thing—in fact, it is a good thing. If you respond to that call with an open mind, you may reap something from the Prayer that you never expected.

There's one motivation for taking up the Prayer that I would discourage, though. Somehow in our day, the concept of "spirituality" has gotten unhitched from actual communion with God—and the fear and trembling authentic contact evokes—and come to be regarded almost as a hobby. Folks who seek spirituality rather than God can give off whiffs of superiority, as if they think they're more elevated than ordinary folks.

Once when I was speaking about the Prayer, a man in the audience commented, "Somehow this seems different from what I usually hear about spirituality. I think the main thing is that it doesn't have that element of narcissism."

The spiritual path of the Jesus Prayer is not one that lends itself to narcissism. The effect of the Prayer is to knock you down in your own mind. Then you discover that it is safe to be knocked down, safe to be humble, because God's love is everywhere, filling the world with his light and life. The Prayer will make you into a child. "Truly, I say to you, whoever does not receive the kingdom of God like a child shall not enter it" (Mk. 10:15). When defensiveness falls away and humility flows in, you become able to love others with the love that God has for them, and even "count others better than yourselves," as St. Paul urged the Philippians (Phil. 2:3).

I am hardly an expert on the Jesus Prayer, but I'd like to help you understand it at least as far as I do. Too many of us spend our days feeling that God is far away, occupied with more important things. But Jesus told us that isn't true; God is so familiar with our bodies that "even the hairs of your head are all numbered" (Mt. 10:30); he is so familiar with our thoughts that he "knows what you need before you ask him" (Mt. 6:8). I hope that through the Jesus Prayer you, too, may learn how to tune that "little radio" to the voice of God, and discover the joy of his infinitely loving presence.

Part One

Chapter One

The Jesus Prayer arose in the early church as a way to practice continuous prayer. When I decided to start using it in my own life, I remembered that St. Paul had said something about "pray constantly," and went to look up that passage.

I was surprised to find that he had expressed the thought in four different places:

> "Rejoice in your hope, be patient in tribulation, be constant in prayer." (Rom. 12:12)

> "Pray at all times in the Spirit, with all prayer and supplication. To that end keep alert with all perseverance." (Eph. 6:18)

> "Continue steadfastly in prayer, being watchful in it with thanksgiving." (Col. 4:2)

> "Rejoice always, pray constantly, give thanks in all circumstances." (1 Thess. 5:16–18)

He must have thought this message was important, because he said it to four different communities—the Romans, Ephesians, Colossians, and Thessalonians. It must have been one of the points he emphasized regularly. And he must have thought it was *possible*. He wouldn't have kept on telling these early believers to "pray constantly" if they were humanly incapable of doing so.

It's not easy to do, though, is it? Many devout Christians have taken a stab at trying to pray constantly, but give up in frustration before long. In my case, I was always discovering that somewhere along the line I had simply stopped praying. When I did persevere, I ran out of things to say. If I tried filling the time by just repeating, "Thank you, Lord," and such, it soon felt hollow. I worried that I was even ruining my ability to pray sincerely, numbing myself by repeating prayers without paying attention.

And, frankly, I just didn't understand how it was supposed to work. How can you be thinking prayers all the time, when you have to think about other things too?

Earlier generations of Christians figured all this out. In the third century, prayerful men and women began to go into the deserts of Egypt and Palestine in order to devote themselves unceasingly to communion with God. (They are known as the Desert Fathers and Mothers, and have the title "Abba" and "Amma.") The desert appealed to them because it eliminated most of those other things to think about, and life was stripped down to the essentials. Extreme deprivation taught self-mastery, and was itself a physical form of prayer.

In the desert, these spiritual athletes experimented with different forms of constant prayer. They recognized that the task was to discipline the wandering mind and focus it on something spiritually healthful, so they memorized the

Scriptures (the Psalms, in particular) and quietly murmured the verses to themselves throughout the day.

Great depths could be found in a single line. Abba Pambo (AD 303–75) could not read, so he asked another desert dweller to teach him a psalm. When he heard the first words of Psalm 39, "I will guard my ways, that I may not sin with my tongue," he asked the other monk to stop and then meditated on that verse alone—for nineteen years. (Asked whether he was ready to hear at least the remainder of the verse, he replied that he had not mastered the first part yet.) Evagrius of Pontus (AD 345–99), on the other hand, listed 487 Scriptures, each of which was to be memorized and brought forth when needed to combat a specific tempta-tion. St. John Cassian (AD 360–435) recommended the first verse of Psalm 70 as the best all-purpose Scripture for those seeking continual prayer: "Be pleased, O God, to deliver me! O Lord, make haste to help me!"

With time, the form "Lord Jesus Christ, Son of God, have mercy on me" emerged as the universal favorite. It echoes the many times people asked Jesus for mercy during the years of his earthly ministry:

"A Canaanite woman from that region came out and cried, 'Have mercy on me, O Lord, Son of David.'" (Mt. 15:22)

The ten lepers "lifted up their voices and said, 'Jesus, Master, have mercy on us.'" (Lk. 17:11–19)

"Bartimaeus, a blind beggar, the son of Timaeus, was sitting by the roadside. And when he heard that it was Jesus of Nazareth, he began to cry out and say, 'Jesus, Son of David, have mercy on me!' And many rebuked him, telling him to be silent; but he cried out all the more, 'Son of David, have mercy on me!'" (Mk. 10:46–48)

"A man came up to him and kneeling before him said, 'Lord, have mercy on my son, for he is an epileptic and he suffers terribly.'" (Mt. 17:14–15)

But what does it mean to ask for mercy? Some people feel uncomfortable with that plea, since asking for mercy over and over could sound like doubting God's forgiveness. Why do we have to keep begging, like a prisoner begging a judge to be lenient?

Take another look at these Scriptures. None are requests for leniency; all are cries for help. The pleas come from people who know that they are needy. Each one appeals to Jesus' compassion, his pity. The need may be for release from an illness, or release from the tyranny of sin. (We could add the tax collector in Jesus' parable, who "would not even lift up his eyes to heaven, but beat his breast, saying, 'God be merciful to me a sinner!'" Lk. 18:13.) In some way we don't immediately understand, healing and forgiveness are linked.

The roots of the Jesus Prayer go back to the early centuries of Eastern Christianity, and we can get a better understanding of what the Prayer means by examining how it works in that native context, and seeing how the Orthodox Church views sin and forgiveness. I am writing this book during Orthodox Holy Week, and just last night attended the service of Holy Unction, in which we consecrated the oil that will be used in anointing for healing during the coming year. In the course of this service we heard seven Epistle and seven Gospel readings, each presenting examples of miraculous healing; we also offered many prayers emphasizing God's compassion. After that, the Gospel Book was held open over the heads of the worshipers, who came forward to be anointed with the newly blessed oil.

Throughout the evening, the theme of healing was interwoven with assurance of forgiveness; we were often reminded that those who are anointed have been forgiven their sins as well. In a mystery, the two go together; God's compassion to heal is his compassion to forgive. We see an example of this in practice, when Jesus says first to the paralytic lowered through the roof, "Your sins are forgiven" (Mt. 9:2), healing his soul in advance of healing his body.

The Eastern Christian tradition lays great stress on God's willing forgiveness. Like the father of the prodigal son, he longs for the sinner's return: "While [the son] was yet at a distance, his father saw him and had compassion, and ran and embraced him and kissed him" (Lk. 15:20). God "desires all men to be saved and to come to the knowledge of the truth" (1 Tim. 2:4). Jesus said that "the Son of Man came to seek and to save the lost" (Lk. 19:10), and "I came not to call the righteous, but sinners" (Mk. 2:17). God spoke these words through the prophet Ezekiel: "As I live, says the Lord GOD, I have no pleasure in the death of the wicked, but that the wicked turn from his way and live; turn back, turn back from your evil ways; for why will you die?" (Ezek. 33:11). Orthodox prayers regularly call God "all-compassionate," "all-merciful," and state, "you alone love mankind." God's love is the only love in the universe worthy of the name. God *is* love, and his forgiveness can be nothing but abundant and free.

So this isn't a question about whether we're forgiven. No, the problem lies elsewhere; the problem is *we keep on sinning*. Sin is in us like an infection in the blood. It keeps us choosing to do and say and think things that damage Creation and hurt other people—and the ill effects rebound on us as well. There can even be *sin* without *guilt*. Sometimes we add to the weary world's burden of sin through something we did in ignorance or unintentionally, for example, by saying something that hurt a hearer for reasons we knew nothing about. Our words increased the sin-sickness in the world, yet we are not guilty for that unintentional sin (though we are still sorry for inadvertently causing pain). Sin can be recognized as a noxious force on earth without having to pin the guilt on someone every time.

In the Eastern view, all humans share a common life; when Christ became a member of the human race, our restoration was begun. The opposite is, sadly, true as well; our continuing sins infect and damage everybody else, and indeed Creation itself. It's like air pollution. There is suffering for everyone who shares our human life, everyone who breathes, even the innocent who never did anyone harm.

The devil is implicated in this pattern. This is a premodern church, and Orthodox Christians retain a practical belief in the devil, one rooted in long experience. The evil one is a tempter, rather than a figure from a horror movie; his goal is to destroy our faith and drag us from salvation. And he loves suffering, especially when it is inflicted on the innocent. That's two-for-one, in his book; he gets to savor not only the tears and agony of the innocent, but also the distress of us not-so-innocent folks who look on helplessly. If he handles things just right, and suggests the right desolating thought at the optimal moment, he might even undermine an onlooker's faith in God.

In the Christian East there is an answer to the problem of evil: "An enemy has done this" (Mt. 13:28). And our own petty sins contribute to his strength.

So we ask for mercy because we are sick with sin, and will go on sinning. Even though we are as confident as beloved children in our Father's compassion, we grieve because we contribute more to the planet's suffering every day. The tragedies in each morning's news were assisted in some small way by yesterday's stupid, selfish, fearful choices. We are helplessly entangled in sin and suffering, and only Jesus' touch will heal us. We cry out with the blind, lame, and paralyzed of his day: Lord Jesus Christ, have mercy on us!

God doesn't need us to remind him to be merciful; he is merciful all the time, even when we don't ask. But unless we make a habit of asking for mercy, we forget that we *need* it. Ego builds a cardboard fortress that humility must, every day, tear down. "For you say, I am rich, I have prospered, and I need nothing; not knowing that you are wretched, pitiable, poor, blind, and naked" (Rev. 3:17). We are piti-able, and God pities us.

With God's merciful help, we begin to heal. Progress is not very discernible in the midst of the fray, but over time it becomes clear that we are indeed fighting off the infection and gradually getting stronger, less fretful, more loving. With the Jesus Prayer, we begin to get some breathing room. We start to be able to recognize the subtle thoughts that lead toward temptation, before it is too late and they overwhelm us. We see and resist them, and every such victory increases our strength to resist next time.

Of course, sometimes we see those temptations and fall anyway. But even failures can work for our good. They induce genuine humility; they help us learn the devil's strategies; and they teach firsthand compassion for fellow sinners.

This process of healing takes a long time. Even as we see reasons for hope, we simultaneously gain better understanding of how far down the roots of sin can go. It would be devastating to see the whole truth about ourselves all at once. Our compassionate Lord brings us along gently, allowing some blissful ignorance. Each layer of the onion is shed at the right time; we encounter the next truth about ourselves when and how we can bear it, as our loving Lord knows best. "I have yet many things to say to you, but you cannot bear them now" (Jn. 16:12).

You can see why, if there was only one prayer you were going to continually offer, one that asked Jesus for mercy would be ideal. The Prayer trains you to adopt the stance of asking for mercy, because that is the posture from which you can best see his face. It's like trying to see a star out your window on a summer night. The leaves of the trees and the neighbors' roofs block your view, but if you lean over just right and crane your neck, you can see it. The Jesus Prayer teaches you how to "lean just right," combining joy, trust, penitence, and gratitude, so you can find yourself in his presence.

Till now we've been talking about learning to sense God's presence, but his plan for us goes even further than that. We don't merely encounter Christ or imitate him, we don't merely become *like* Christ; we actually become one with him, saturated body and soul with his life. It will be for us as it was for St. Paul: "For to me to live is Christ" (Phil. 1:21), and, "It is no longer I who live, but Christ who lives in me" (Gal. 2:20).

Have we gotten used to taking such words as pious metaphor? In the Jesus Prayer tradition, they're simple Bible truth. The whole point of salvation is restored union with God. Christ came to rescue us from our bondage to sin and the devil ("The reason the Son of God appeared was to destroy the works of the devil," 1 Jn. 3:8), and we are now free to grow in union with him.

What could "union with God" mean, in practice? It meant something different to me at one time than it does now. Before my family and I joined the Eastern Orthodox Church, in 1993, we were members of a mainline liturgical church. I liked learning about the historic faith (I'd gotten a seminary degree alongside my husband, a pastor) and did a good bit of reading in classic Western Christian spirituality. From the perspective I gained there, I associated talk about union with God with images of the mystic saints, floating above the ground and dizzy with ecstatic visions. That was the sort of stuff you left to professionals—the "don't try this at home" category of spirituality.

So it was surprising to find that, in the Eastern Christian tradition, union with God is the goal for everyone. It is God's will for every Christian, and, through their preaching of the gospel, for every human being. The purpose of this earthly life is to be saturated with the life of Christ. Everything flows from that, every work of art and act of courageous witness, every theological insight and every effort to help the poor. The idea is that God will fill people with his Son's life, and then they will accomplish his work in the world. It works better that way, actually. The other way round, when people set out to do things *for* God under their own steam, leads to disappointment, conflict, and wasted effort.

This process of assimilating the presence of God is called *theosis* (pronounced "THEH-o-sees"). *Theos* means "God," and as a cloth soaks up water by osmosis, we are saturated with God through theosis. This indwelling presence heals, restores, and completes us, preparing each of us to take up the role in his kingdom that we alone can fill.

Progress in theosis is a gift of God, not won by any effort, of course. But you can make yourself available to such a blessing by practicing spiritual disciplines, such as observing the fast days in the church's calendar (in the Orthodox Church, this means keeping a vegan diet) and saying the Jesus Prayer. Such resources are like the workout machines in a health club, the ones every serious athlete will use. People who are making progress share some common characteristics, too: good self-control when it comes to the appetites, absence of anger, ample humility, kindness, and diligence in prayer. But some folks have a more sober quality, while others are full of joy; there isn't any one personality type. If anything, the indwelling Christ enables each person to be more himself than he was ever able to be before.

I've noticed that men are particularly drawn to Eastern Christian spirituality. Men, I think, are starving for a form of Christianity that will ask something of them. They're hungry for a challenge—a *clear, straightforward* challenge, that is. I did an informal survey not long ago, asking male converts what had attracted them to Orthodoxy. I was surprised at how many men voiced gratitude, not just for the rigor of Eastern spirituality (*challenge* was, in fact, the most-used term), but also for the fact that expectations are set forth clearly, with no secret meanings that they have to figure out. Men are glad to do hard things, as long as they have a clear idea of what they're supposed to do. (In this gratitude for clarity I heard an echo of all the frustrated husbands who have said to their wives: "I'm not a mind reader—just tell me what you want!")

When this concept of theosis is unfamiliar, it is hard for a reader to make any sense of it; it may even sound alarming or kooky, or like empty, well-meaning piety. Once I had given a talk about the Jesus Prayer at a college, and as I left the podium a student was waiting to ask a question, ready to jot down my answer. He asked, "Are there any case histories?" I was perplexed by the question, so he tried again: "Has anyone ever tried to do this?"

I didn't say, "Well, *I'm* trying to do it." Instead, I suggested a couple of names he could look up on the Internet (St. Seraphim and Motovilov, in case you want to look them up, too). But the moment impressed me with how hard it must be to grasp what I'm talking about from an isolated lecture or a book.

The Jesus Prayer isn't designed to be learned that way. Historically, it has been passed on face-to-face, from one Christ-loving person to the next, down the generations from the time of the Desert saints. It is learned in a community of fellow believers, all of whom are aware of their need and sin, trying daily to resist temptation better and love God more. It should be individually coached or tutored by a spiritual mother or father who knows you through and through, who loves you, holds you accountable, and is able wisely to adapt the classic teaching to your unique struggles. In short, the Jesus Prayer is meant to be learned in the midst of a living community, where you can see numerous examples of what it looks like when ordinary people are doing it and encouraging each other. When you can see real folks doing it, it is a lot easier to grasp, and seems a lot more possible.

Theosis is a vast and daunting goal even to imagine, so there's something distinctively, sweetly Christian about using a prayer that is so simple. There have been plenty of other religions that taught convoluted mystical procedures for union with God, but for Christians it is as straightforward as calling on our Lord and asking him for mercy. As you form the habit of saying this prayer in the back of your mind all the time, it soaks into you, like dye into cotton, and colors the way you encounter every person and circumstance you meet.

There's the answer to the practical question I had a while back: how can you think about the words of the Prayer all the time, when there are so many other things you have to think about? In the same way that you can have a meal, go on a trip, or visit a museum with a friend. You could do all of those things alone, but if you take a friend with you, it won't hinder your enjoyment. You may get even more out of it, because your friend's presence enhances your awareness, and you see things through his eyes as well. When you see everything alongside that best of friends, Jesus Christ, your encounters with the world and everyone and everything in it are transformed.

Chapter Two
TERMS, CONCEPTS, AND CONTEXT

The Jesus Prayer has been treasured in the Christian East ever since its birth in the desert, more than 1,500 years ago. There have been periods when the Prayer was very popular, and other times when it was not much practiced; at some points, it seemed as if only a few monks on Mt. Athos, the renowned center of Orthodox spirituality in northern Greece, were keeping the practice alive. (Orthodox men's and women's monasteries are still a good place to find the Prayer's most diligent practitioners.) But because the Prayer is so simple, it's accessible to anyone, lay or ordained, educated or illiterate. Over the centuries, uncountable numbers of believers have come to know God's constant nearness by practicing this fluid, continual remembrance of Jesus' name.

In the eighteenth century, two monks gathered historic writings on prayer and monastic life, ranging from the fourth to the fourteenth century, into an anthology called the *Philokalia* (that's Greek for "love of the beautiful"). Other works on the Prayer have been written in the centuries since, the best known being an anonymous memoir called *The Way of a Pilgrim*, which appeared in Russia in the nineteenth century. When a translation of that work was published in Europe in 1925, it gave Western Christians their first encounter with the Prayer as a living practice. (A character in J.D. Salinger's 1961 book *Franny and Zooey* is shown reading *The Way of a Pilgrim*, which further made it known.)

If you read classic works about the Jesus Prayer (I make some suggestions at the back of the book), you'll encounter some new terms. Sometimes the phrase "prayer of the heart" is used interchangeably with "the Jesus Prayer." They don't mean exactly the same thing, however. "The Jesus Prayer" refers to the specific words of the Prayer, and the Prayer as a prayer discipline and historic entity. "Prayer of the heart" refers to the *action* of the Prayer, something that may occur, by God's grace, within a person who diligently practices the Prayer.

At first the Prayer is just a string of words repeated, perhaps mechanically, in your mind. But with time it may "descend into the heart," and those who experience this will be attentive to maintain it, continually "bringing the mind" (the nous, that is) "into the heart." We'll explore the terms *mind* and *heart* in the next chapter, but for now, keep in mind that these don't correspond to "reason" and "emotion"; both terms have different definitions in the Christian East.

But this "descent into the heart" does include reference to the physical heart (or the general region of the heart within the chest). This blending of matter and spirit can be surprising to Western Christians, but it came naturally to the earliest Christians, who inherited from ancient Judaism an expectation that God is present throughout Creation. "Do I not fill heaven and earth? says the LORD" (Jer. 23:24).

"Prayer of the heart" occurs when the Prayer moves from merely mental repetition, forced along by your own effort, to an effortless and spontaneous self-repetition of the Prayer that emanates from the core of your being, your heart. You discover that the Holy Spirit has been there, praying, all along. Then heart and soul, body and mind, memory and will, the very breath of life itself, everything that you have and are unites in gratitude and joy, tuned like a violin string to the name of Jesus.

This "descent" is a gift of the Holy Spirit, not something you can force. So you may say that you are practicing the Jesus Prayer, but it would sound boastful to say that you are practicing prayer of the heart.

Another term you'll hear is *hesychia* (pronounced "heh-see-KEE-ah"). In biblical Greek this word means "silence," "quiet," "stillness," or "rest." It is not an empty silence, but one marked by respect and awe. I think of Job, who said, when confronted by God's majesty and power, "I lay my hand on my mouth" (Job 40:4). A holy person who has progressed far in acquiring this inner stillness may be called a "*hesychast* elder." *Hesychast* silence makes room for profound, attentive listening. With time, the Prayer quiets and unifies the scattered, wandering nous, so that it can focus on God's presence in simplicity, with love.

As I begin defining terms associated with the Jesus Prayer, I am faced again with how much more there is to explain. There are some basic differences between Eastern and Western Christianity. It probably sounds absurd even to speak of Western Christianity as a single entity, if you picture the vast diversity of faith expressions that grew up in Europe and America. But from the Eastern perspective, these Western versions of Christianity all have a strong family resemblance. As Metropolitan Kallistos Ware writes in his classic book, *The Orthodox Church*, "In the west it is usual to think of Roman Catholicism and Protestantism as opposite extremes; but to an Orthodox they appear as two sides of the same coin."

It shouldn't be surprising, really, that the two great geographic realms of Christendom would develop different characteristics. They lived different histories; they grappled with different controversies, fought different wars, asked different questions, produced different art, and developed different forms of government and very different cultures.

What's more, they read different versions of the Scriptures. The East continued to use the Greek text (including the Greek Old Testament produced by Jewish scholars about 250 BC; that's the version St. Paul quotes from). But the West adopted a Latin translation of Old and New Testaments in about AD 400. A language shapes a worldview; every language maps the world in its own way.

In composing this chapter, I've found it frustrating to try to make a thumbnail sketch of Orthodox Christianity; it's hard even to know where to *start*. If I choose one element, another starts waving its hand in the air and saying it needs to go first. The Jesus Prayer is the most intimate and powerful prayer discipline of Eastern faith, and I was reluctant to write about it at all; for several years I kept declining the invitation. (I'll tell you what changed my mind later on.) But let's take a few pages to try to note some of the characteristics of Eastern Christianity.

Perhaps the first, and most telling, point to make is that *spirituality* is not a word used much in Orthodox contexts (of course, it gets used by Orthodox writers in the West). The reason is that *everything* is "spirituality." Christian Orthodoxy is itself a spiritual path, rather than an institution or set of propositions.

What's more, all the elements of this path are integrated in such a way that, to a practitioner, it is seamless. From the outside Orthodoxy must look exuberantly chaotic, but from the inside it is a closely coordinated collection of wisdom (some elders term it a "science") about how to pursue *theosis*. Every element serves that purpose. I asked a knowledgeable, widely read friend what one word he would choose to describe Orthodoxy. He replied, "*Organic.*"

Nor does Eastern Orthodoxy have the range of devotional practices seen in the West. There is not an array of monastic orders, each with its own emphasis or mission. There is really only one "program" of spiritual healing, and within it the Jesus Prayer holds a unique role.

The basis of inclusion in this program, as far as I can tell, is effectiveness. Every element—icons, hymns, prayers, fasts, architecture, you name it—must provide help in progressing toward theosis. Basically, it has to *work*. The program does work, satisfyingly, so it gets passed on from one generation to the next, without provoking a restless desire for updating. (It works if you work it, of course. Just belonging to a church is not enough, as belonging to a health club is not enough if you only drive by and wave.) And it appears to work for people of all cultures. It has taken root everywhere from Wales to Finland to India, from Ethiopia to Alaska, maintaining the same characteristic flavor no matter where it goes. Even Eastern churches that are not in communion with each other, due to ancient or modern squabbles, evidence the same spirituality. They all hearken back to a common, ancient faith.

Thus, in the East there is a single, united form of spirituality, aimed at the clear goal of theosis. It is a process of being healed and strengthened, body and soul, and freed from compulsion to sin. Body as well as soul, you see; this process is not merely spiritual. While contemporary Christians know that God is not absent from the material world, we do have to keep reminding ourselves about it. It wasn't the same with the early Christians, because this was a question they had to face frequently in debate. Their opponents were often representatives of a philosophical-religious view that the world of matter is worthless, if not evil, and the mind alone is pure enough to encounter God. The proposition that God could come to earth in the form of an ordinary human body was, to them, both preposterous and revolting.

Christians opposed that position by defending the reality of Christ's Incarnation, insisting that he had taken on a real human body and hadn't just conjured an illusion. His entry into human life began the healing and restoration of that life. What's more, if God could take on human form, our bodies are capable of bearing God's presence in return. An ordinary human body can literally become a "temple of the Holy Spirit" (1 Cor. 6:19). That can sound alarming—wouldn't God's presence destroy my feeble frame?—but Eastern Christians frequently draw an analogy to the burning bush. Just as Moses saw that the bush burned with God's fire but was not consumed, so God's presence can fill us while preserving—even completing—our embodied personhood.

An ancient analogy is to a sword placed in a furnace. The blade increasingly takes on the properties, or "energies," of fire, as it becomes radiant with light and heat—and yet it remains the same length of metal. As quantum science discovers more about the mysterious energy at the core of all matter, I keep thinking over St. Paul's marvelous words: "All things were created through him and for him. He is before all things, and in him all things hold together" (Col. 1:16-17).

Oddly enough, the word energy occurs frequently in St. Paul's letters; he says, for example, "God is *energon* [energizing] in you, both to will and to *energein* [energize] for his good pleasure" (Phil. 2:13). *Energy* is a word we imported into English directly from the Greek. But there was no equivalent for this word in Latin, so in his masterful translation of the Bible, St. Jerome (AD 347–420) used *operare*, that is, "operate" or "work." When the Bible began to be published in English, its translators stood at the end of a thousand years of devout reading, preaching, and studying the Bible in Latin translation. Our English Bibles refer to God "working," not "energizing," but isn't there a difference? If we hear that God's energy is within us, then union with him becomes more imaginable.

And if God is present, "energizing" in the physical world, then miracles can still happen. It is another mark of the premodern character of Eastern Christianity that it continues to hold a simple early-church faith in the reality of miracles. It is a trust that is well rewarded. (My husband

uses the oil from the Holy Unction service to anoint the
sick, and one year learned that three hospital patients,
all thought to be on their deathbed, had subsequently
recovered enough to go home.) In this regard, the East is
much like the many Western Christian traditions that still
pray for, and expect, God's intervention in everyday life.

"The prayer of a righteous man has great power in its
effects" (Jms. 5:16), and miracles are often the fruit of
holiness. Stories abound, even today, about *hesychast* elders
who are associated with healings, supernatural gifts of
knowledge, Eden-like relationships with the environment
and animal life, and many other kinds of miracles. If you
make a pilgrimage to a holy site or monastery and meet
privately with such an elder, she may unfold to you your
history and innermost struggles. (This is called "soul-
reading" or "clear-sight.") A friend of mine once described
to me how much trepidation he felt before making such a
pilgrimage. But as he thought about the healing power of
truth, and how God would only give such knowledge if it
would bring him freedom in Christ, he began to dare to
hope for it. He spread wide his very long arms, and said
with a beaming smile, "Read me!"

This is surely another one of those things that best
make sense if you encounter them "in action" in a living
community. People don't need only facts and information;
they also need to see how other people work with and regard
such things. We learn best by watching other people. At a
fancy luncheon, you watch the hostess to see which fork
she picks up next. In spiritual matters, you watch the old-
timers and listen to them, and gradually learn how it all fits

together. This is why the ancient churches tell and retell the lives of the saints.

Another thing: I noticed that among Orthodox Christians there was a more serious attitude toward spiritual disciplines than I had been used to. (I'm talking about those Orthodox who actually practice the faith, of course.) This rests on the assumption that *life* is serious, salvation is serious, and in every moment we must decide anew to follow Christ.

It's not that there is any question about God's love or his forgiveness, as we've said; our salvation was accomplished on the cross. "In Christ God was reconciling the world to himself" (2 Cor. 5:19). But we retain this terrifying freedom: we are still free to reject him. Judas's tragic story is a sobering example. The end of our own story is not yet written, and every day exposes us to new temptations. The devil knows our weaknesses, probably better than we do, and "prowls around like a roaring lion, seeking someone to devour" (1 Pet. 5:8).

This is why there is in Orthodox spirituality a quality of *urgency*. We don't assume that we have already made it to the end of the race, but "press on," as St. Paul said:

> That I may know him and the power of his resurrection, and may share his sufferings, becoming like him in his death, that if possible I may attain the resurrection from the dead. Not that I have already obtained this or am already perfect; but I press on to make it my own, because Christ Jesus has made me his own. Brethren, I do not consider that I have made it my own; but one thing I do, forgetting what lies behind and straining

forward to what lies ahead, I press on toward the goal
for the prize of the upward call of God in Christ Jesus.
(Phil. 3:10–14)

Again, this has nothing to do with a lack of confidence
in God's willingness to save us. But we don't dare have
confidence in ourselves. "Pride goes before destruction, and
a haughty spirit before a fall" (Prov. 16:18). It's a perspective
that keeps us on our toes.

On the first three days of Holy Week we offer the service
called Bridegroom Matins, and sing this hymn:

> The Bridegroom comes at midnight,
> And blessed is he whom he shall find watching,
> But unworthy is he whom he shall find heedless.
> Beware therefore, O my soul,
> Lest you be weighed down with sleep,
> And be given over unto death,
> And shut out of the Kingdom.
> But rouse yourself, crying,
> "Holy, holy, holy are you, O Lord."

This theme of urgency or watchfulness runs all through
Orthodox spirituality. It originated in the Scriptures, of
course; if you look again at St. Paul's exhortations to constant
prayer, above, you'll notice how he adds admonitions to
"keep alert with all perseverance" and to be "watchful in
[prayer] with thanksgiving." St. Peter prefaced his words
about the devil prowling like a lion with the warning, "Be
sober, be watchful." The hymn's image of the bridegroom's
midnight arrival, and the calamity awaiting the unprepared,

comes from Christ himself. I wonder how any Christians ever got to the point of *not* feeling this urgency. Christ told us: "What I say to you I say to all: Watch" (Mk. 13:37).

I'm going to try to stop there, though many other hands are still frantically waving. I said above that the single word to describe Eastern Christianity is *organic*—that everything fits together and has its role to play. From that you can deduce that some Orthodox find it hard to imagine how people could benefit from the Jesus Prayer if they take it out of context. You need *all* the elements, they would say, including participation in the Orthodox sacraments (called "mysteries" in the East) and acceptance of Orthodox theology.

In 1957, Metropolitan Anthony Bloom (1914–2003), whose small book *Beginning to Pray* is well loved, gave a lecture to the London Guild of Pastoral Psychology. He was talking about the physical effects of prayer of the heart, and spoke of the necessity of accurate doctrine for those who practice the Jesus Prayer. The passage seems rather strong to us today:

> As for dogma, it is of major importance. The doctrine of the Church, as well as expressing its living knowledge of God and the spiritual life, defines strictly the believer's attitude towards the divine world. Any error in dogma, however slight it may appear to our clumsy experience of the things of God, reveals some deviation from the spiritual order, just as any wrong path in this realm leads infallibly to dogmatic insensibility and error.

Dogma is thus the touchstone and objective foundation of any life of asceticism and contemplation, of which it is also the school; assimilated by the patient, humble effort of the whole being, it leads man beyond the realm, vast as it is, of philosophical knowledge, then on from affirmative cataphatic theology, to introduce him into the realm of true theology, silent, personal knowledge of God in the fervent silence of the whole created being—the realm of the true apophatic theology, which characterizes the Eastern Church.

People don't air out interdenominational differences these days as much as they used to, perhaps for the very good reason that Christianity is so widely criticized that we should publicly link arms whenever we can. The differences still exist, though, and are worth knowing about, since they could affect your experience with the Jesus Prayer. We may think: how can it possibly matter what doctrine you hold, as long as you truly love and follow Christ? Metropolitan Anthony points out that a difference in doctrine means a different understanding of "the divine realm" and "the spiritual order," an alternate view of reality itself. It would be like trying to drive through Tennessee using a map of Maine.

And some Orthodox elders hold that self-directed use of the Prayer is, in fact, dangerous, potentially leading to delusion, then to possible insanity or demonic possession. Here's a characteristic passage from Elder Porphyrios (AD 1906–91), a contemporary Greek elder:

You must have the guidance of a spiritual father. Prayer of the heart is impossible without a spiritual guide. There is danger of the soul being deluded. Care is needed . . . . [I]f you don't get into the right order, there's a danger of your seeing the luciferic light, of living in delusion and being plunged into darkness, and then one becomes aggressive and changes character and so on. This is the splitting of the personality. . . .

[If] desire is enkindled, not by your good self, but by the other self, the egotistical self, then undoubtedly you will see lights, but not the light of Christ, and undoubtedly you will begin to experience a pseudo-joy. But in your outward life, your relations with other people, you will be ever more aggressive and irascible, more quick-tempered and fretful. These are the signs of a person who is deluded. The person who is deluded does not accept that he is suffering from delusion. He is fanatical and does harm.

However, Elder Porphyrios is mostly thinking of people who harbor prideful fantasies of being a certified mystic, able to wield supernatural powers and demonstrably superior to ordinary folks. Such people are in grave danger, for they will eventually encounter artificial versions of the experiences they're hankering for (whether demonic or self-induced), and from there may fall into an ironclad, continually self-validating delusion. Yes, there are people who crave that sort of extraordinary experience, but I hope you're not one of them. Stay humble and you will be safe. "O LORD, my heart is not lifted up, my eyes are not raised too high; I do not occupy myself with things too great and too marvelous for me. But I have calmed and quieted my soul, like a child quieted at its mother's breast; like a child that is quieted is my soul" (Ps. 131:1–2).

Elder Porphyrios lays great emphasis on having a spiritual guide, but how do you find one? The classic answer is to inquire at an Orthodox men's or women's monastery; you might even find well-experienced clergy or laity at a local Orthodox church. But they may be at a loss to advise someone who wants to learn the Jesus Prayer apart from the rest of the program, since from the inside it all seems interdependent, every part necessary.

It is said that "Saying the Jesus Prayer will teach you how to say the Jesus Prayer," because practicing it can set in motion a process of spiritual healing that seems to unfold all by itself. It works like the scattered seed in Christ's parable, which "sprout and grow" though the farmer "knows not how" (Mk. 4:27). It may be that the Prayer is best able to work this way when practiced within its organic context, where everything, from the hymns to the visual arts to the sermons to the Scripture readings, reinforces the distinctive view of the "divine order" and "spiritual realm" (in Metropolitan Anthony's words) in which the Jesus Prayer arose.

It may be that this curiously self-germinating process isn't as readily experienced in another context. And yet, if you are open and humble, how could it hurt? Why not just ask Jesus for mercy? Certainly, every Christian could say this prayer, and benefit. They may not experience the upper reaches of psychological and spiritual transformation that the holy elders have written about through the centuries, but, if the Prayer is offered sincerely, it will bless them all the same.

Perhaps it is like cutting a rose in a garden and placing it indoors, in a vase. It will still be beautiful and fragrant, but it won't be exactly what it was; it no longer draws its life from the garden. Speaking of my own experience, when I was reading the classic spiritual literature before my journey East, I sampled many different forms of prayer and meditation—just mixing and matching, seeing what felt right. In the process, I ran across the Jesus Prayer and gave it a try a couple of times, but I never could get it to stick. This is all in the hands of God, of course.

I know that I am not qualified to write about the Jesus Prayer at the level it deserves; it's fair to say that a beginner like me should not write about it at all. But I came to think that an inadequate book might be better than none, for I could see that the use of the Prayer is spreading, severed from its original context. While searching the Internet, I come across a site that teaches that the "Jesus Prayer" consists of repeating the name "Jesus" only and no other words. I see a review of a book in which the author reports that his experience with the Jesus Prayer was enhanced when he combined it with Buddhist meditation. I run across an all-purpose prayer website that offers this invitation: "Enjoy the inspirational words of the Jesus Prayer. Pray using these free online words."

So I decided to go ahead and do the best I can. Love Jesus, love him with all your heart, and ask him to guide you. Your experience of the Prayer will be your own, not like anyone else's. And if you cling to humility, you will come to joy.

Chapter Three

HEART, MIND, AND THE "LITTLE RADIO"

As I began to write this book, I piled up all the prior books and writings that I could find on the Jesus Prayer, and I noticed one thing: they're pretty short. It's a short prayer, and the way to do it is to just keep saying it over and over. Those instructions could fit on the back of a shampoo bottle:

1. Pray "Lord Jesus Christ, Son of God, have mercy on me."
2. Repeat.

But if that's all you know, you'll soon run into trouble. You can try to force your mind to keep going over and over those words, like a gerbil on a wheel, but it's going to get pretty tedious.

The hard part is to *mean* them. The hard part is to pull together all your attention, though it kicks like a toddler, and focus it on the Lord, and then humbly ask for his mercy. Learning to actually mean the Jesus Prayer, from ever-deepening regions of your heart, is what makes the practice so challenging.

What makes it so rewarding, however, is that you can begin to sense the responsive presence of the Lord. Then the words of the Prayer start to make sense—they start to feel like the natural thing to say.

It's like saying, "I love you." An adolescent can try to imagine how it will feel when he finally speaks those words to his true love, but no matter how much he practices, they remain mere words. When the moment comes, the experience of his beloved's presence is so overpowering that the words flow naturally, and seem like the only possible thing to say. They are no longer theoretical and portentous, but have become evidence of something piercingly real but inexpressible, vast beyond words.

One of the biggest handicaps we have in prayer, though, is that we aren't sure it's actually *possible* to sense the presence of God. That's the first thing we have to clear up, the assumption that we don't have the equipment necessary to perceive God's presence. If we want to perceive or sense something, we employ the standard equipment: sight, touch, hearing, and so on. But we don't expect God to manifest himself by such means. Talk of that kind of overt experience of God serves mostly to make the person talking look like a kook.

Apart from that, we think we have the two modes of active awareness. There's the "head," the intellect or human reason; we think of it as the side that is accurate and realistic, though a bit cold. In the opposite corner we have the "heart," which we see as an unstable swamp of emotions, though nevertheless the source of our finest impulses.

We like to say, "We need both head and heart." When talking with atheists, we're inclined to grant that they have "head" on their side, that their approach is more objective, or even scientific. We'd agree that when we experience the presence of God, it is a matter of our emotions, arising from the "heart."

Thus we function under the assumption that there are two aspects of human consciousness, reason and emotion— and there's the problem. If we believe that God cannot be experienced through human reason, what's left for such contact to be but emotional? Thus, when you say you had an experience of God, it seems to mean that you had emotions about God.

It frustrates me that Christians so readily give way when this question comes up. If I told you I experienced going to the dentist, you would assume that I actually went to the dentist. You wouldn't think I had some emotions that felt just like going to the dentist. It's only when we Christians begin talking about God that we get uncertain about how real it is, and start agreeing with nonbelievers that "experience" means "emotional projection."

Once you start looking at it, though, this whole division into "head" and "heart" becomes less certain. If you think about your own inner life, you'll notice that "head" and "heart" aren't really polar opposites. In practice, they muddle up so much that they're impossible to separate. Emotions slip around our thoughts and shape them; "rational" is cousin to "rationalize." The way we want things to be can powerfully affect our ability to see how things really are.

And thoughts provoke strong emotions; it can be argued that *all* our emotions are reactions to thoughts. When you feel sad or excited, it's generated by something you're thinking about. Even when we can't put our finger on the cause of an emotion, somewhere behind it is foggy, perhaps suppressed, thought.

This insight, in fact, has produced a breakthrough in the treatment of psychological illness. It seemed that people could talk for years about their experiences and feelings, yet gain little improvement. More recently, some therapists have been trying a different approach: they encourage their clients to focus on their thoughts, rather than their emotions, with the aim of observing and challenging the erroneous ideas that provoke their anxiety or depression. The Prayer, as we'll see, utilizes a similar approach, calling us to be vigilant about the thoughts we harbor, scrutinizing them and rejecting lies. We know who the "father of lies" is (Jn. 8:44).

So, in practice, neither head nor heart is as airtight as we generally presume. This polarized picture of "head" and "heart" doesn't correspond to Scripture, either. There the word *head* is never used as a synonym for "reason." A glance at a Bible concordance will show that it always means either the physical head on a body or a person in authority, and never the rational intellect. Now, every culture certainly gets an opportunity to observe that head injury affects the ability to think, and from that must draw some conclusions about the cogitating function of the brain. Nevertheless, in the world of the Bible, the head is never associated with thinking.

Confusingly enough, the authors of Scripture, and Jesus himself, presume that thoughts arise instead in the *heart*. As Jesus said, "For out of the heart come evil thoughts"

(Mt. 15:19). The association of the heart with thinking appears consistently throughout the Scriptures (as seen, for example, in Gen. 6:5; Ps. 33:11, 139:23; Jer. 4:14; Mk. 7:21; Lk. 2:35; and Heb. 4:12).

Feelings of tenderness and compassion, which we think of as synonymous with "heart" (as in, "That guy has a big heart") are instead associated with the contents of the abdomen and lower body: bowels, kidneys, womb, and the "inner parts" in general. (Here are some examples, though in contemporary translations the reference has often been euphemized: Mt. 15:32, 18:2, 20:34; Mk. 1:41, 8:2, 9:22; Lk. 1:78; 2 Cor. 6:12, 7:15; Phil. 1:8, 2:1; Col. 3:12; Philem. 1:7, 12, 20; 1 Jn. 2:17.)

So what used to be assigned to bowels and heart is now located in heart and mind. Apparently, over the last several millennia, everything's been rising.

Sometimes translators take it upon themselves to elevate the site of this inner attention just a little farther. The ancient Greek version of Psalm 16:7 reads, "I will bless the Lord who has given me understanding; in the night also my kidneys instruct me." The King James Version says, "My reins also instruct me," *reins* being an archaic term for "kidneys." The Revised Standard Version says, "In the night also my *heart* instructs me," while the New American Standard Version renders it, "My *mind* instructs me in the night." In another century, maybe we'll read, "My hat instructs me"!

When we say "mind" or "head," we think of the active process of reason—the part of us that builds theories and crafts arguments. The Greek word for that faculty is *dianoia* (pronounced "dee-ah-NOY-ah"). We don't have a word in English for the mental function when it goes the other direction, the part of us that confronts life firsthand, which perceives or comprehends. Since there's no word for it, we don't know it exists.

But it does exist, and in the Greek Scriptures, there's a word for it. When you see the word *mind* in an English Bible, the Greek word that lies behind it is usually *nous* (pronounced "noose"), and it doesn't quite equal our concept of "mind."

What it does mean was hard for me to figure out. When I began reading works about prayer from the Christian East, I noticed that *nous* was frequently left untranslated. This suggested that the English language just doesn't have a good equivalent. As I traveled around the country giving talks, meeting people who were trying to acquire the Prayer, they'd sometimes ask, "Do you understand what *nous* means?"

So I tried to nail it down. As I read through a lengthy book on Eastern Orthodox spirituality, I took an index card and wrote down the definition of nous, as best I could grasp it, every time I ran across the term. At the end of the book, I had six definitions.

But gradually I came to see that the kind of "mind" intended by nous primarily indicates the *receptive* faculty of the mind, what we might call "the understanding." For example, "[Jesus] opened their nous to understand the scriptures" (Lk. 24:45). This is the part of the mind that engages directly with life, which comprehends and takes things in.

What's more, it is a *perceptive* faculty, capable of recognizing truth. Not in the sense of arriving at a logical conclusion at the end of an argument; the nous instead perceives truth in a direct, intuitive way. When you hear "the ring of truth," it is your nous that does the resonating.

Another function of the nous is the ability to hear the conscience, that "little voice inside." You know you're not just talking to yourself, because it's telling you things that you would rather not hear. The nous keeps a line open to the voice of God and, even in a person who has wandered far from faith, a flickering link endures in the form of the (perhaps unwillingly) listening conscience.

So the nous enables a direct experience of God, apart from reason and emotion. But here's how we get tangled up: if you have an experience of the presence of God, it's quite likely you'll have thoughts and emotions *afterward*. But if your language doesn't provide a way to express the experience itself, and all you have words for is the emotions and thoughts that resulted, you're likely to assume that the experience itself was a function of your intellect or (more likely) emotions.

That's not the case. There really is an experience in the first place.

The nous is primarily a receiver—it's the "little radio" I lacked words for, just after my conversion. It is placed in us so that we can perceive God's voice and presence. But in the Fall the nous was damaged—the usual term is "darkened"— and no longer perceives accurately. It doesn't much *want* to listen to God. It constantly craves stimulation. If you tried to keep track of your thoughts for even one hour you'd be amazed at their restless range. A contemporary elder said that the nous is like a dog that wants to run around all the time.

The nous needs healing. It doesn't perceive things clearly, due to damage caused by the fog of sin that affects us all. Healing of the nous involves getting rid of the erroneous thoughts and emotions that cloud our minds. We need to have a clear-eyed view of reality, if we want to encounter God. Reality is God's home address.

But the nous doesn't want to focus on the Prayer. When you start to pray, it gets restless and begins to jump around, trying to find anything at all to think about. The strangest thoughts pop in. In Greek, these attacking thoughts are called *logismoi* (pronounced "law-yiz-MEE"); a single thought is a *logismos*. (You'll hear such words pronounced in various ways. On the advice of Metropolitan Kallistos Ware, I am using mostly modern Greek pronunciation.)

Our thoughts about the world are what control us, and much of the time they are off base. You may be governed, unaware, by misunderstandings you picked up as a child. Thoughts about other people are especially likely to be erroneous and self-damaging. These false thoughts make us fearful, greedy, and vindictive; they undermine our trust in God, and make us subject to every kind of human dysfunction. The "darkened" nous is easily deluded, and self-deluded. The process of spiritual healing cleanses the nous, like cleaning grime off the glass of a lantern.

Here is where the Prayer comes in. With regular use, it begins to open up a little space between you and your automatic thoughts, so that you can scrutinize them before you let them in. It builds a foyer, so to speak, where incoming thoughts must wait to be examined before being granted admittance.

This healing is a lifelong process, and your self-serving thoughts, in particular, are adept at disguising themselves; they may escape detection for many long years. But over time you will discover that some very old automatic thoughts are just plain wrong, and you don't have to think them anymore. As the nous is gradually healed, its perceptions become more accurate, less agitated. You begin to acquire "the nous of Christ" (1 Cor. 2:16). "Be transformed by the renewal of your nous," said St. Paul (Rom. 12:2).

So the Prayer has a great deal to do with your thoughts, your interior mental life. It will end up sending you, like an explorer, through the jungle of your own psyche. You will always be discovering something new about yourself, something you need to correct or move out of the way. In his book *The Sign of the Cross*, Andreas Andreopoulos described this process. "The individual's spiritual battle . . . is fought on many levels of the self, and is successful when the deepest parts of the personality have come to also reflect the spiritual struggle that the Cross attests. The Desert Fathers were very aware of this. Most of the ascetic literature essentially represents a sophisticated psychological journey into the self, with Jesus as the compass." And also, I would add, the goal.

You can see why there is so much emphasis within Orthodoxy on having an elder, a spiritual guide. But many of us must, of necessity, take up this journey without an elder, and do so with fear and trembling. We must never forget that our heart is a nest of trickery and self-deception. "The heart is deceitful above all things, and desperately corrupt; who can understand it?" (Jer. 17:9). It

is unable to perceive clearly: "a veil lies over their heart"
(2 Cor. 3:15; this is another case where the Greek says "heart"
but the English translation substitutes "mind"). It is possible,
in the absence of an elder, to be led by the Holy Spirit; but it
is wise to keep seeking for the one who can guide you with
wise words and protect you with ardent prayer.

Be certain that there is no help in intellectuality, or in
having read a great number of spiritual books. A common
tragedy is for a person to get diverted from the path of
prayer onto the path of *talking about* prayer. A sign that
the enemy has penetrated far into the mind of such a one
is that she becomes smug and no one can tell her anything.
No attribute of intelligence or cleverness will save you, no
ability to phrase things deftly, no elegant symmetry of your
ideas. Just keep crying out for mercy. Only humility breaks
in pieces all the machinery of the enemy.

We are like the prodigal son, who comes home sick and
injured. It was his own sins that brought him to that state,
and he can't blame anybody else. He repents because he now
sees the truth. He doesn't need to repent in order to earn
the father's forgiveness; the father had already forgiven him,
and rushes forward to embrace his child without waiting to
hear an apology. "While he was yet at a distance, his father
saw him and had compassion" (Lk. 15:20).

God loves us like that; he isn't waiting for us to coax him
into forgiving us. But, like the son, we have to recognize
the truth about our wounded condition. We must recognize
that we *need* the father's love. The darkened nous doesn't
readily grasp this. We see that something is wrong with the
world, but don't perceive that the wrongness is tangled up

with, and enabled by, our own thoughts, words, and deeds. Realizing the truth about ourselves, our complicity in the world's brokenness, is the first step of healing.

The prodigal son had that moment of clear insight; "he came to himself" (Lk. 15:17). Then he knew that he needed to go home and tell his father that he was sorry, and beg for a second chance.

Did the son have an emotional experience? No doubt about it; but it was the fruit of a moment of intellectual clarity. His understanding was enlightened, his nous recognized truth, he became rational; he was at last put in touch with reality.

The root meaning of *repentance*, or *metanoia* (pronounced "meh-tah-NOY-ah") in Greek, means that sort of change of mind: gaining insight, coming to your senses, seeing the truth. Jesus said, "You will know the truth, and the truth will make you free" (Jn. 8:32). It is hard to face truth when you feel alone in the universe, with a distant God who doesn't know your name and may be sulking over something you did years ago. You can feel brave enough to know and admit this truth only when you are sure you are loved, because "perfect love casts out fear" (1 Jn. 4:18).

A God who is remote and scary and judgmental, taking offense at things that (we think) have nothing to do with him, is hard to love. The natural reaction is instead to deny the sins, or rationalize them away, or compare yourself to someone else whose behavior is worse. A barrier of mistrust lies between a person and this kind of God.

This Eastern Christian path is not particularly concerned with morality or good behavior, surprisingly enough; it is concerned with a *relationship*. The Pharisees achieved high levels of good behavior, but if that was enough, Jesus would have chosen his apostles from their ranks. No, they were pretty on the outside and rotten on the inside, like "whitewashed tombs" (Mt. 23:27). Jesus consistently put the emphasis on the state of the inner person. He said, for example, that the eating of "unclean" foods does not defile a person, but rather what comes out of the mouth, because that rises from the heart: "evil thoughts, murder . . . false witness, slander" (Mt. 15:19).

It's that transformed heart and nous he's looking for. After that healing, good behavior flows out naturally. So this approach does not disregard morality; Jesus said, "You, therefore, must be perfect, as your heavenly Father is perfect" (Mt. 5:48), and "Unless your righteousness exceeds that of the scribes and Pharisees, you will never enter the kingdom of heaven" (Mt. 5:20). But moral behavior is worthless without a transformed mind and heart. To get good fruit, you must "make the tree good" (Mt. 12:33).

That's the kind of repentance God is looking for—a change deep inside us, one that signals our desire to restore the relationship and be conformed to his likeness. This healing is premised on the confidence that God already sees all the way through us. He sees everything we ever did, knows our every thought, and yet loves us, even enough to die for us. So there is no reason to hide and make excuses; he already knows it all, anyway. Remember the story in the Gospels, in which Jesus was at supper at the home of Simon the Pharisee and a penitent woman came in and wept at his feet, washing them with her tears. As Jesus told Simon, she had great love, because she knew she had been forgiven much.

Those who think of themselves as fairly decent and upright are going to have a harder time achieving repentance. Such a person doesn't see that God has had to forgive very much in them. As a result, they can't be sure that his love is strong. Those who are forgiven much, love much; they know they are receiving much love.

The practice of the Prayer will initially take some serious self-discipline, but it gradually grows sweet, and then irresistible. The hope of protection from your own vicious or self-hating thoughts is alone a strong impetus to persevere. Day by day the healing advances, and continual immersion in Christ's presence becomes your goal. One day you will find that the Prayer is starting up within you on its own, like a dearly loved melody. And then you will know the blessing that St. Paul gave the Philippians, "the peace of God, which overflows all the nous, will keep your *kardia* [hearts] and *noema* [thoughts] in Christ Jesus" (Phil. 4:7).

Part Two

GETTING STARTED

QUESTIONS AND ANSWERS

Orthodox elders would say that you must first get your house in order. If there is major ongoing sin in your life, then cut it out. At least *want* to cut it out; cultivate repentance by thinking on the glory and compassion of God, and your squandering of that love. It is actually better to repent sincerely of a sin, and to go on struggling even though you fall, than to have never had the temptation in the first place. Jesus said, "There will be more joy in heaven over one sinner who repents than over ninety-nine righteous persons who need no repentance" (Lk. 15:7). The sinner who doesn't repent is another matter.

Look for a spiritual mother or father. Many Orthodox Christians turn to their parish priest for this, while others seek one at a men's or women's monastery. If you can't find one, embark on the Jesus Prayer with whatever resources you can gather, but retain an extra measure of caution about your own capacity for spiritual pride. You're still bound to make some mistakes, but at least you won't be surprised when you do.

Attend worship; be part of a worshiping community. Receive the sacraments (in Orthodoxy, called "Holy Mysteries"). Go to confession, if that is part of your spiritual heritage. In the East, confession is viewed more as an aid to spiritual healing than as the discharging of sin-debts. There is great solace in speaking your sins out loud, and hearing the priest say these words:

> May God who pardoned David through Nathan the
> prophet when he confessed his sins, and Peter weeping
> bitterly for his denial, and the sinful woman weeping
> at his feet, and the publican and the prodigal son, may
> that same God forgive you all things, through me a
> sinner, both in this world and in the world to come,
> and set you uncondemned before his terrible Judgment
> seat. Having no further care for the sins which you
> have confessed, depart in peace.

Pastor Richard Wurmbrand, who was imprisoned by
the Communists in his native Romania, describes an aged
priest he met behind prison walls, Fr. Surioanu. Other
prisoners were drawn to this priest, and regardless of their
religious background, Fr. Surioanu would listen as they told
him about their sins, and he would assure them of God's
forgiveness.

Pastor Wurmbrand wrote, "The more I told him sins, the
more beautiful and loving became his face. I feared in the
beginning that when he heard about such things he would
loathe me. But the more I said bad things about myself,
the more he sat near to me. And in the end he said, 'Son,
you really have committed plenty of sins, but I can tell you
one thing. Despite all of these sins, God still loves you and
forgives you. Remember that He has given His Son to die
for you, and try one day a little bit, and another day a little
bit, just to improve your character so it should be pleasant
to God.'"

Pray, fast, and give alms. Eastern Christians continue the
first-century practice of fasting on Wednesday and Friday,

and during Great Lent and other fast periods during the year. This is not an absolute fast, but mostly a matter of abstaining from meat, fish, and dairy. Give a tenth of your income, a tithe, to your church, if you can; if not, give whatever percentage you can afford and work up to (and then beyond) the tithe. Give alms to charity as well. Give wisely.

Serve those in sorrow and need, in person if at all possible, for personal contact will affect you in ways not gained through merely writing a check. In our culture we are disposed to approach social needs with an eye to efficiency, expecting to pool expertise and resources, form an organization, and execute a program. The achievements of such organizations are so substantial that what we do privately tends to look insignificant. But the Scriptures presume that all charity is taking place in the context of personal relationships.

Our word *charity* comes from the Latin *caritas*, corresponding to the Greek New Testament word *agape*, which means "long-suffering, self-giving love." This is the kind of love we are supposed to show to the poor and needy. In fact, we should give that love even to those who are not poor and needy; we're supposed to love everyone, even our persecutors (Lk. 6:27–28).

So practice agape in every context (and it does take lots of practice). Every person you encounter gives you a God-appointed opportunity to die to self. The six or ten people you deal with every day are meant to furnish your own personal "Roman Coliseum," where you can battle against self-will till your last breath.

The elders are unanimous that curbing self-will, dying to self at every opportunity, is essential to spiritual healing and growth. This kind of self-discipline is called asceticism, after the Greek word for the training an athlete undergoes when preparing for a marathon, or an apprentice follows in learning her craft. Asceticism is not hatred of the body. The body's inborn, natural desires are good when they operate as God intended, but in practice they tend to overrun their boundaries. Sometimes the mind even exceeds the body's desires, as when I eat something because it says "chocolate" on the wrapper, even though it doesn't taste particularly good. As the nous is cleansed and strengthened, it will be more able to guide the body rightly.

It is standard advice to avoid excessive sleeping, and to leave the table before you feel full. Overeating is widely recognized as a factor that undermines the ability to maintain constant prayer. Continually stretch yourself with small challenges in all areas of your preferences and desires, cutting away little pleasures that you think you can't live without. But don't go overboard with a sudden, possibly prideful, attempt at excessive asceticism. This seems to tempt young men more than it does other people. "One needs to get used to moderation gradually," says Abp. Anthony Golynsky-Mihailovsky (AD 1889–1976).

Expect that you will have sorrow, and that you will suffer injustice; expect this, and it won't shatter your faith. Believe firmly that all your joy is with Christ, and you will be able to bear it if other sources of joy prove temporary, or are never found at all. And keep in mind that our sins assist the evil one and contribute to the world's ongoing tragedy, so it is fitting that we bear part of the resulting burden.

Jesus said, "In the world you have tribulation." You will, he promises; just take a deep breath, and accept it. In this world, pain will visit everyone sooner or later.

But Jesus didn't stop with that thought. He went on, "But be of good cheer, I have overcome the world" (Jn. 16:33). Pain may be inevitable, but it is also temporary, and that alone is a comforting thought. Pain is mandatory, but misery is optional.

Humility is of more value than the greatest asceticism. One day, as the desert monk St. Macarius (AD 300–391) was returning to his cell, the devil attacked him swinging a scythe, but was unable to wound him. The devil complained, "Macarius, I suffer a lot of violence from you, for I cannot overcome you. Whatever you do, I do also. If you fast, I eat nothing; if you keep watch, I never sleep. There is only one way in which you surpass me: your humility. That is why I cannot prevail against you."

Pride can be hard to detect because it disguises itself in innumerable ways. It appears most often in relationships, because pride springs up when comparing yourself with other people. If you instead compare yourself with God, and with what God is calling and enabling you to be, sincere humility is not so hard to feel.

One clue to pride is anger; often, when we get angry, it is because pride has been dealt a wound. Avoid anger at all costs. The Desert Fathers warn more frequently against anger than against sexual sins, because anger poisons the soul. As the saying goes, "Anger is an acid that destroys its container."

Consider yourself too immature to handle even so-called "righteous anger." More frequently, this turns out to be self-righteous anger. Jesus was able to roar into the temple and throw tables over, but he had certain spiritual advantages that we don't. Our popular entertainment routinely invites us to indulge in vicarious vengeance, and presents it as a noble and satisfying pursuit. But "you did not so learn Christ" (Eph. 4:20), for our Lord could have called down "more than twelve legions of angels" (Mt. 26:53) and orchestrated a very cinematic vengeance, if that was his way of doing things.

It's a long list, and no one is going to do it all perfectly. Still, Jesus said, "You, therefore, must be perfect, as your heavenly Father is perfect" (Mt. 5:48), so we should keep pressing onward. Do whatever you can to make your soul "pleasant to God," as Fr. Surioanu so gently recommended. Every failure can be turned to gold, if it increases your humility.

Q: *AND THEN WHAT?*
HOW DO I BEGIN THE PRAYER ITSELF?

The goal is to gain the Jesus Prayer as an unceasing prayer offering to God. It sounds lofty, but as with so many of the worthwhile things in life, a large part of meeting your goal depends on just showing up. Do what you said you'd do, whether you feel like it or not. Simple perseverance eventually succeeds, like water wearing away a stone.

In basic terms, what you're attempting to do is to form a new habit. In this case, it's the habit of praying without ceasing. Yet, due to the restlessness and distractibility of our minds, an attempt to start out praying right now and never stop is going to be met with disappointment.

It's impossible to start doing anything *all* the time. You have to start with doing it *some* of the time. Set aside a regular time for practice every day, and as the habit takes root you can encourage it to spread out from there, like vines escaping the boundaries of a garden.

The first thing to decide is when you're going to have this practice time. Perhaps you already have a daily "quiet time," during which you pray, read the Bible, offer intercessions, and so forth. You can add to that time an extra ten or fifteen minutes for repeating the Jesus Prayer. You could even undertake one prayer session in the morning and the other in the evening, and set the Prayer going once again as you drop off to sleep. However, don't set your sights too high; establish goals that you can reasonably keep. You can always add more later.

I found that the single biggest advance in my prayer life came when I expanded from my single mid-night prayer time and added brief "prayer stops" during the day at morning, noon, sunset, and bedtime. Those prayer times were never for me as deep and rich as the mid-night session, but the mere act of breaking up my routine and turning toward God in the midst of busy preoccupation was itself a valuable aid.

This pattern of stopping for prayer several times a day is mentioned in the oldest of Christian documents outside the

New Testament, the Didache (pronounced "didd-ah-KEE"; it's also called "The Teaching of the Twelve Apostles"). The Didache was written in the late first century, perhaps about the same time as the Gospels of Matthew and Luke. It's an interesting text because it details what Christians do and don't do, and how they worship (it's a brief text; you can find it online). At one point, it provides the words of the "Our Father," and says that Christians should pray it three times a day. (It also mentions fasting on Wednesday and Friday.) So, if you are presently doing all your praying at one time of the day, you could use this opportunity of adding the Jesus Prayer to rearrange things, and divide your praying into two or more sessions. See if you benefit from that; it certainly improved things for me.

But maybe you don't already have a dedicated daily prayer time. You'll need to establish one, if you want to practice the Jesus Prayer in a formal and disciplined way. But some people do without a regular time to practice the Jesus Prayer, just employing it spontaneously during the day; we'll get to that option below.

When I first began trying to have a daily prayer time, decades ago, I decided that at 5:00 PM every day I would stop and pray for five minutes. *I thought I was going to jump out of my skin.* I hated it. I hated having to be still and focus on nothing but God, even for five minutes. So I know how hard this can be at first, and you have my sympathies. It does get easier with practice.

St. Gregory the Great (AD 540–604) said, "There is a great difference, dearly beloved brethren, between corporal and spiritual delights, in that the former, when we are without them, enkindle in the soul a strong desire to possess them, but once they are attained, they quickly satiate us. Spiritual pleasures, on the contrary, when unattained, produce a certain aversion; but once we taste them, the taste awakens desire, and our hunger for them increases the more we taste them."

If you've successfully added a good habit to your life before, you might be able to identify what helped you then and apply the same lesson here. I once read an article about the best way to form a new habit; the author had evaluated hundreds of "self-change techniques" and identified the three most effective methods. First, monitor yourself, and keep track of whether you meet your goal (for example, every day that you practice the Prayer, check it on your calendar). Second, commit to someone else that you will report your success or failure (a spiritual elder is ideal, but you could track success with a friend or family member instead). Third, make the new habit a convenient part of your daily routine. "Pin it" to something else that you do every day. Do you read the news every morning? When you sit down with the paper or at the computer, close your eyes and say the Jesus Prayer first. If you read your e-mail every day, say the Prayer after you sit at your desk but before you open your e-mail account. Pick something that is already an established habit, and embed this new practice into what you're already doing.

Be sincere in your prayers, whether you're saying the Jesus Prayer, participating in a church service, or saying private prayers at home. Don't ever let prayer become mere rote repetition. St. John of Kronstadt writes, "When you pray, the Lord will give you according to your heart. If you pray with faith, sincerely, with all your heart, not hypocritically, the Lord will reward you accordingly. And on the other hand, the colder your heart, the more doubting and hypocritical, the more useless will be your prayer—and more: so much the more will it insult the Lord, who seeks to be worshiped 'in spirit and truth'" (Jn. 4:23).

Some people elect to undertake their daily practice of the Jesus Prayer as they're drifting off to sleep. This sounds like a good plan, because you won't feel pressured to hurry up and do something else, and you will be soothed and relieved of worries as you prepare for sleep. But personally, I resisted that option because I was afraid I'd forge an association between saying the Prayer and getting sleepy. I was hoping (still am hoping) one day to really be able to pray without ceasing, and if my ingrained experience of the Jesus Prayer was pillow time, I would not learn how to employ it while alert and functioning. That was my thinking, anyway; I could be wrong. Whenever you do set up your daily prayer time, there's no reason you couldn't also use the Prayer as you're heading off to sleep.

The benefit of making this an ingrained habit will last all your life, outlasting, perhaps, even your conscious aware-ness. People who care for the elderly, and pastors who pray beside a deathbed, know that those who have journeyed far into dementia still respond when they hear something famil-iar that expresses their faith. A friend's mother was often afraid because she no longer recognized her surroundings, but would become quiet and be comforted when my friend opened the Bible and read favorite passages aloud. When my spiritual father, Fr. George Calciu (AD 1925–2006; he was, like Pastor Wurmbrand, a survivor of torture in Communist prisons), was in his last hours, though he had long appeared insensible to those around him, he tried to sing along when a favorite hymn was begun, and struggled to lift his right hand to make the sign of the cross.

The things we lay down firmly in our memories *matter*. They endure. If you take the words of the Jesus Prayer and "write them on the tablet of your heart" (Prov. 3:3), on the day when you are far away on the gray sea of Alzheimer's, the Prayer will still be there, keeping your hand clasped in the hand of the Lord.

A nun had been assigned to care for an elderly monk with advanced dementia. One day his babbling was of a kind that was distressing to her. Suddenly he broke free, as it were, looked her in the eye and said, "Dear sister, you are upset because of what I am saying. But do not fear. Inside, I am with God."

The Jesus Prayer is rightly called a prayer discipline, because it entails hard work. St. Paul spoke of laboring with the Galatians "until Christ be formed in you" (Gal. 4:19). So I hope you're not disappointed to learn that there is no trick or short cut to being able to pray constantly. What you have to do is: pray constantly. The Jesus Prayer offers a framework, a way to begin doing it. It's encouraging to remember that it has met the test of time, and proven itself over more than fifteen hundred years.

Q: HOW MANY TIMES SHOULD I SAY THE PRAYER DURING ONE PRACTICE PERIOD?

I've been referring to ten or fifteen minutes for practicing the Prayer, though you could spend more or less than that. The Jesus Prayer was in use for many, many centuries before clocks and wristwatches were common, so it wasn't measured in minutes. The usual way to keep track was by aiming to say a certain number of repetitions, typically in quantities of a hundred. One hundred repetitions will take ten or fifteen minutes, depending on how fast you say them. (As you get more adept at maintaining your attention, you'll likely want to say the Prayer more slowly, and a set of a hundred might take up to half an hour.)

You can say more than a hundred repetitions, of course. I found that, for me, the first hundred was necessary just to clear the mosquitoes out of the room. When I began saying the Prayer regularly, in 1995, I started out with three hundred repetitions each night. But when I met my spiritual father, Fr. George Calciu, and told him that this was my custom, he had me reduce it to one hundred repetitions, saying that he did not think it was good to make great numbers of repetitions.

My prayer partner Ina, however, ran across the advice always to say three hundred repetitions, and to say them as fast as possible. I mention this as an example of the diversity of teaching you may encounter. In some cases, this occurs because advice has been tailored to a particular spiritual child. In other cases, it is because each elder has his or her own preferred way of doing things. I imagine golf pros likewise have preferred stances and grips that they teach to all their students.

At the opposite extreme from these quantities of a hundred or so, the narrator of *The Way of a Pilgrim* meets an elder (in Russian, a *starets*; in Greek, a *geron*) who instructs him to say the Prayer for extraordinary quantities of repetitions. The elder starts him at three thousand repetitions a day and raises it by steps to twelve thousand. I have not heard of anything like that quantity elsewhere, though, and today it would be considered excessive even for monks and nuns.

So, have the aim of saying the Prayer "all the time," but discipline yourself daily to do it for a certain number of repetitions, or for a specific period of time, in order to form the habit.

Q: *WHEN I DO SPEND TIME PRACTICING THE PRAYER, HOW DO I KEEP TRACK OF THE NUMBER OF REPETITIONS?*

In ancient times, the desert monks kept track by removing pebbles or seeds from a sack one by one, or by counting the notches on a wooden staff, or the knots in a woolen cord. A traditional story tells of a monk who made a knot in a cord for every repetition of the Prayer, but while he slept, the devil would come and untie all the knots. An angel appeared and showed the monk a special sort of knot, one formed of seven intricate overlapping crosses, and this one the devil was unable to untie.

St. Pachomius (AD 292–348), one of the foremost Desert Fathers, is credited with being the first to use a prayer rope, a loop of wool made with those elaborate knots; it has become the most common way of keeping track of the Prayer. A prayer rope is usually made of black wool, though you sometimes find them in other colors and materials. Prayer ropes come in standard lengths. The shortest, of thirty-three knots, fits around the wrist like a bracelet, while lengths of fifty, one hundred, and even three hundred knots can be wrapped around your wrist or kept in a pocket. (If wearing it on your wrist provides a glow of pride at your visibly profound spirituality, keep it in your pocket.) While you're praying, hold the prayer rope in your left hand, moving your fingers along the knots in turn. Keep your right hand free for making the sign of the cross.

Some prayer ropes end with a tassel that is said to be for wiping away tears. An element of Eastern Christian faith is an expectation that when you really grasp reality deeply, when you see how much God loves the world and cares for it, and how many people fight against him and each other and go down captive into hell, and how your own stupid sins show contempt for his love and hinder his work, you will weep. For some saints, tears become a constant companion, and this is spoken of as "the gift of tears."

This is a complex matter, though, because humans are complex, and tears may also spring from despair, or frustration, or be put on artificially in a pageant of spiritual pride. Even authentic tears tend to evolve, moving from profound penitence to gratitude and joy. In any case, they should not be accompanied by emotionalism and sobbing, which would be self-indulgence. And some people simply are not disposed toward tears, no matter how authentic their repentance. If you have no tears, ask God to deepen your repentance. "There does not escape your notice even one tear, O Redeemer, nor a fraction of a teardrop," says St. Simeon the New Theologian (AD 949–1022).

You don't have to use a prayer rope; you can certainly say the Prayer without one. Some people find it helps them concentrate, however, if they have something to do with their hands. When I presented the Jesus Prayer at a weekend retreat where no prayer ropes were available, several women told me that they were using the links of their bracelets or wristwatches as a substitute.

Personally, I've had the habit of counting off the prayers on my fingers when I can't use my prayer rope—for example, while I'm driving. If I assign three prayers to each finger, and go through both hands three times, I am getting into the neighborhood of one hundred repetitions (or so they tell me; I was never good at math). I recommend this to audiences, but some people seem to find it very confusing to do it this way. One person told me that this advice could be harmful to people with Obsessive-Compulsive Disorder, who should not be invited to start counting things. I never thought of that.

Greeks call a prayer rope a *komvoskini*, Russians call it a *chotki*, and others know it by different names. My friend Jeannie taught me how to make them, but I didn't continue to do so because the knots are so very complicated, and even when I made them correctly they were lumpy and all different sizes and too far apart. Jeannie makes them *perfectly* (she was taught by a monk from Mt. Athos). But the other reason I didn't go on trying to make them was because Jeannie told me, as she had been taught, that you have to say the Prayer continually while making the knots (it takes about ninety minutes to make a thirty-three-knot rope); if your mind wanders, you must undo all the knots and start again. When my prayer is shallow and cold, I am comforted to think of the prayers of the person who first held this prayer rope as he or she made these knots, and filled them up with prayers.

Q: SHOULD I HAVE A SPECIAL PLACE FOR PRAYER IN MY HOME?

Most Orthodox Christians have an "icon corner" at home. This is usually a corner in one of the home's main rooms, perhaps the living room or dining room. It usually occupies the corner (or stretch of wall; it doesn't have to be a corner) on the east side of the room; one of the earliest Christian traditions is to face east while praying, since the Lord will return "as the lightning comes from the east and shines as far as the west" (Mt. 24:27). If there isn't a suitable place in those rooms, a place in a hallway or bedroom will do just as well. (If you place another icon of Christ so that it is visible when you watch TV, you will find it has an effect on what you watch. Put one beside your computer monitor, too.)

In the prayer corner there are typically at least two icons, one of the Lord and one of the Virgin Mary (known to Eastern Christians as the *Theotokos*, pronounced "theh-o-TOK-os," which means "birth-giver of God"). The icon of Christ goes on the right and the icon of the Theotokos on the left—that is, she is placed at Christ's right hand ("At your right hand stands the queen," Ps. 45:9).

The icon of Christ should be one that shows him blessing with his right hand while holding a Gospel Book in his left; this depiction is known as the Pantocrator (the Ruler of All). The icon of Mary should depict her holding the infant Christ. This icon shows Christ at his first coming, at his birth in Bethlehem, while the Pantocrator icon shows him at his second coming, when he comes to judge the earth. In an Orthodox church you will always see examples of these icons on the right and left of the center door of the iconostasis, framing the altar, where Christ meets us in the present moment.

Once you get a couple of icons, you're going to get more. They just seem to accumulate. Group these around the anchoring icons of Christ and the Theotokos. You will eventually want an icon of the saint who is your patron, because he or she is your special prayer partner. (You'll still go directly to the Lord with your prayer requests; you ask your patron saint to pray too, just as you ask earthly friends. The very ancient expectation that we have prayer partners in heaven arose from the early Christians' profound certainty that Christ has conquered death.) This might be a saint who shares your name or first initial, or whose feast falls on the day you were born, or is simply a saint with whom you feel a particular connection. (The other day I got an e-mail from a man who said he was a recovering alcoholic, and had formed an attachment to St. George as an elder brother and prayer partner in Christ. St. George is depicted slaying a dragon, he said, and his alcoholism was like a monster in his life.)

You may want icons of the saints of friends and family members whom you pray for, and icons depicting events in Scripture or church history, or other saints you've grown close to. There are a few Internet stores that sell paper icons laminated onto wooden plaques; if you would like to commission a hand-painted icon, a clergyman at a local Orthodox church may be able to help you find an iconographer. (Icon painting is a spiritual discipline in itself, carried on in prayer and fasting. The process involves layering the paint upward from dark to light, in dozens of nearly translucent layers, so it is quite time intensive.) I've often used an Internet browser to search for image files of a saint by name, and then printed out the nicest high-resolution file I could find.

In Eastern cultures there is more kissing than we're used to in the West; icons are greeted with a kiss (either directly, or conveyed by fingertip), which is called "venerating" an icon. As you arrange your icons, keep in mind that you may want to be able to reach them for veneration.

It's handy to have a shelf in your icon corner to hold prayer books, incense, candles, a prayer rope, a Bible, or anything else you'd like to have handy. You can get small, decorative shelves ready-made at most department and home improvement stores. For our "big" icon corner downstairs, we used the niche of what had been a built-in bookcase in the living room. Our "small" icon corner upstairs utilizes the top of a bookcase as a shelf, with icons arranged on the wall above.

Having said all that about an icon corner, it might not be the place where you end up practicing the Jesus Prayer. You stand at an icon corner, as Eastern Christians generally do for prayer everywhere (standing throughout most church services), but the traditional advice about the Jesus Prayer is to practice it seated. There's a reason for that, which we'll get to below, when we consider the role of the body in prayer.

Q: *WHERE AM I SUPPOSED TO GET THIS STUFF— ICONS, PRAYER ROPES, AND SO FORTH?*

Orthodoxy is such an embodied faith that there are many such items in use in everyday practice. Since you can't get them at Wal-Mart, or even at your local Christian bookstore, most Orthodox churches have a small ministry that offers them for sale. This is typically a corner of the parish hall, perhaps just a table in the corner, where the wares are laid out for sale after services, and a parishioner stands nearby to advise and make change.

This ministry is usually called the church "bookstore," and books make up a large percentage of the offerings. These are likely to be published by one of the few Orthodox publishing houses, or by smaller presses specializing in, for example, books that were originally published in another language in one of the Orthodox home countries. The translations may be uneven, and the books won't be as polished as you're used to from American publishers, but I've come to find that unpolished, noncommercial quality itself to be charming.

In a parish bookstore you'll also find prayer ropes, prayer books, crosses and other jewelry, icons laminated onto wooden boards of various sizes (rarely, you may find hand-painted icons; usually you have to commission those), incense nuggets and disks of charcoal to burn them on, candles of beeswax and candles in glass votive holders, calendars indicating the fasts and saints' days, note cards with Orthodox images or prayers, and any number of other items. You can find all this online, too, but if such things are unfamiliar, you might like to examine them firsthand.

Q: *SHOULD I PICTURE CHRIST LOOKING AT ME, OR ANYTHING LIKE THAT? OR SHOULD I KEEP LOOKING AT AN ICON OF HIM WHILE I PRAY?*

No, that's one thing on which the tradition is very firm: do not picture anything. Do not use your imagination. Just point yourself toward Christ, toward encountering him firsthand, without making pictures in your mind, and let go of any pictures that suggest themselves.

I know this can sound contradictory, since we've gone to some trouble to surround ourselves with icons. But icons are a reminder of heavenly realities; they are not those realities. You might collect photos of someone who is your hero, but if you had an opportunity to meet that hero you wouldn't take the photos along and keep gazing at them all through the conversation. In the Jesus Prayer, we are trying to remain in direct contact with God, and such images can lure us instead into *thinking about* God.

The priest who is now my spiritual father, Fr. Gregory, told me that he finds it hard to deflect all the images that meet the eye if praying with eyes open; yet, when he closes his eyes, his mind begins supplying endless quantities of stored images. (That doesn't happen to me, but I pass it on to anyone who might find it useful.) He found that praying with eyes *almost* shut helped him find a middle way, where images don't arise.

Recently I gave a talk about the Jesus Prayer on a college campus, and mentioned this emphasis on withdrawing the mind from imaginative images. A student asked, somewhat indignantly, whether that meant that "there is no room for the operation of the Holy Spirit in the Orthodox Church." I replied that, if it really was the Holy Spirit, it would have nothing whatever to do with your imagination. About the most dangerous thing you could do, in fact, would be to set your imagination free, and then believe that whatever it told you was a message from God. Since it is possible to encounter God in reality, there is no need for fantasy.

Christian fiction, movies, and other forms of storytelling seem to us vitally important today, and some beautiful and inspiring works are the result. But there was much less of this in ages past. The stories earlier Christians told mostly came from the Bible and the lives of the saints, and they believed these stories were true rather than fictional. Imaginative works mostly took the form of expanding on actual events, such as picturing what else the angel might have said to Mary when he came to announce the birth of a Son, or the argument the good thief had with the cherub assigned to guard the gate of paradise, who hadn't gotten the memo about the change in admission policy. (A seventh-century Syriac hymn imagines this dialogue in somewhat humorous detail; you can find it by doing an Internet search for "cherub" and "thief"). But there doesn't seem to have been much composing of fiction or fantasy. It's funny that we now feel such a strong need for made-up stories. I'm a movie reviewer and love that art form, but it does seem like contemporary humans spend a lot more time in imaginary worlds than previous generations of Christians ever did.

So, in the Jesus Prayer you don't try to picture anything, and now that I've been Orthodox for a while, the kind of meditation where you're invited to picture Jesus in your mind, and walk up to him and ask a question, seems to me—I'm sorry—truly awful. It seems insulting; Jesus is not your sock puppet. But it also seems unwise, because imagination is always one step removed from reality.

I once attended an event where the speaker told us that, as a Christian, he is a Platonist; he believes the world we inhabit is only a shadow of heavenly reality. So, when we bring the gospel to friends and neighbors, he said, we must insist to them that this world we live in is not the real world, and that after death all this illusion will be dispelled and we'll at last experience reality. When he sat down, the worship minister got up and invited us to pray, saying, "Now let's imagine that Jesus is really present with us. Let's picture what it would be like if he was actually here." And all that time I'd been thinking he really *was* there.

Q: *WHAT IF I DON'T WANT TO INCLUDE FORMAL REPETITION OF THE JESUS PRAYER IN MY DAILY PRAYER TIME? WHAT IF I DON'T EVEN HAVE A DAILY PRAYER TIME?*

We should set the horse firmly before the cart: the goal of saying the Jesus Prayer is not to say the Jesus Prayer *perfectly* for fifteen minutes a day. The goal is to pray constantly, and the only reason for practice sessions is to lay a foundation of habit and familiarity for feeding the remainder of the day. If you don't feel called to spend time in formal practice, you could and should use the Prayer anyway, as you follow your everyday course. (Metropolitan Kallistos Ware calls these the "fixed use" and the "free use" of the Jesus Prayer.) Using the Prayer spontaneously, in all circumstances, brings the Lord into your life in a vivid way. Every task is done in his presence and with his help. Every encounter takes place under his loving gaze.

So, pray at all times, or at least at all the times you think of it. You can "pray constantly" apart from the Jesus Prayer, too. Sometimes we have more specific things to pray about, things we need to name; if so, it is right to converse with the Lord freely about everything on our mind, simply, like a child. It is all right to pray for help in finding a parking place. If it concerns us, it concerns him.

But over the years, our concerns become less anxious and self-centered, and we are able to loosen our grip on what we think we need to have. Priorities shift. If it concerns him, it will concern us. The Jesus Prayer provides a way to maintain a fluid connection through the day, as we listen to hear his will.

I've found that, if I forget to pray for a while, when I realize it I'm reluctant to start up again because I feel scared and guilty. I hear a thought, "He's going to be really angry. He'll say, 'Where were you?'" I've found that it helps to recognize that as a typically lying thought, and head on back anyway. When I get back, he's never angry with me. Funny how that still comes as a surprise, though we've heard the parable of the prodigal son a thousand times.

St. Isaac of Syria (d. ca. AD 700) says, "Sit in the presence of the Lord every moment of your life, as you think of him and recollect him in your heart. Otherwise, when you only see him after a period of time, you will lack freedom of converse with him, out of shame; for great freedom of converse is born out of constant association with him."

St. John Cassian wrote a very appealing passage on how he applied his constant prayer (in his case, not the Jesus Prayer, but the second verse of Psalm 70) as he met the various circumstances of his day. His first sentence could be mine as well: "I am affected by the passion of gluttony." If it tastes good, I want seconds. I rationalize: if I eat now, I won't be hungry later. I rush to help myself before the voice of moderation can make itself heard. At those times, I have to cry: "Lord Jesus Christ, have mercy on me!"

After an episode like that, a voice needles me, criticizing my pointless self-indulgence, reminding me of the effect only a few extra pounds has on my available selection of clothing. When it is too late to do anything about my gluttony, nagging thoughts surround and batter me. Lord, help me, and protect me from my own foolishness. "Lord Jesus Christ, have mercy on me!"

I don't want to open my e-mail account in the morning. It brings mail from friends and strangers all over the world, and though this is mostly a blessing, some of it is argumentative and exhausting. Lord, go before me and govern the mail I receive. Give me love for those who write to me. "Lord Jesus Christ, have mercy on me."

Another writer, a friend, has been recognized and honored. Why wasn't it me? "Lord Jesus Christ, have mercy on me."

I overhear a discussion of politics, and smart-aleck comebacks flood my mind. Dear Lord, help me to resist entanglement in things that I cannot influence or control. "Lord Jesus Christ, have mercy on me."

The phone rings, and it is a lonely person who likes to talk for a long, long time. Feelings of dutiful compassion conflict with more honest feelings of resentment. Lord, give me your love for him, for I have none of my own. "Lord Jesus Christ, have mercy on me."

In the waiting room of the auto repair shop the TV is tuned to the afternoon yelling shows. I hate hearing the things they say. I don't understand why they value money and possessions the way they do, and why they are haughty and vindictive toward parents, children, and friends. How have we become so venal and contemptuous? How could people drowning in this environment be rescued? I look at that obese, cocky, shouting woman and, feel at a loss. Sad and bewildered, I pray, "Lord Jesus Christ, have mercy on me."

While reading the Bible, a verse opens up in a way it never had before, and a beautiful substructure of meaning appears that brings tears to my eyes. In gratitude, I pray that my inconstant mind will retain this understanding. "Lord Jesus Christ, have mercy on me."

While reading the Bible, "sleep glues my head to the sacred page" (in St. John Cassian's appealing phrase). My daily allotment of Scripture is pitifully small in comparison with the range of magazines, websites, and books I linger over. Forgive me, Lord. It looks like after all these decades you have truly made very little progress in me. "Lord Jesus Christ, have mercy on me."

Now sleep has fled, and for several nights I lie in unblinking, unthinking repose, utterly bored and empty. Be my light in darkness, O Lord. "Lord Jesus Christ, have mercy on me."

At coffee hour after church, I look around the parish hall and feel guilty. As the pastor's wife, the *khouria* (pronounced "khoo-rih-yeh," it means the parish's mother, as the priest is its father), I should be on the front line of compassion, but every face I see reminds me of my failure. When we have the Rite of Forgiveness every Lent, I ask each parishioner to forgive me for annoying or neglecting them. Then I go right out and do exactly the same thing for another year. I know how to exhibit superficial niceness, but of authentic love I have none; and how many people in this room do better than me! "Lord Jesus Christ, have mercy on me!"

I can look back and see that some habitual temptations, at one time very persistent, no longer trouble me. Thank you, dear Lord. Preserve in me this small beachhead. "Lord Jesus Christ, have mercy on me."

Thinking further on the victories you have won in me, a warm, comfortable feeling begins to spread. I am not like I used to be, and I am also not like a lot of other people I could name, either, those who waste their time on trifles and rarely pray. "God, I thank thee that I am not like other men" (Lk. 18:11). Dear Lord, rescue me before I drown! "Lord Jesus Christ, have mercy on me!"

St. John Cassian concludes:

> When you wake let it be the first thing to come into your mind, let it anticipate all your waking thoughts, let it, when you rise from your bed, send you down on your knees, and thence send you forth to all your work and business, and let it follow you about all day long. This you should think about, according to the Lawgiver's charge, "at home and walking forth on a journey" (Deuteronomy 6:7), sleeping and waking. This you should write on the threshold and door of your mouth, this you should place on the walls of your house and in the recesses of your heart, so that when you fall on your knees in prayer this may be your chant as you kneel, and when you rise up from it to go forth to all the necessary business of life it may be your constant prayer as you stand.

Q: *WHAT FORM OF THE PRAYER SHOULD I USE?*

The standard form of the Prayer is "Lord Jesus Christ, Son of God, have mercy on me." Many people add to the end, ". . . a sinner." This is not one of the more ancient forms of the Prayer, but it can be very helpful in learning that stance of combined repentance and gratitude. The addition of "a sinner" comes from the prayer of the Publican in Jesus' parable, who "would not even lift up his eyes to heaven, but beat his breast, saying, 'God, be merciful to me a sinner!'" (Lk. 18:13).

A few people pray, "Lord Jesus Christ, Son of the *living* God . . ." This additional word comes from St. Peter's confession, "You are the Christ, the Son of the living God" (Mt. 16:16). I found the best fit for me was to leave out the center phrase, but I wouldn't want it any shorter than that. I hope you will know what I mean when I say that the name of Jesus has inherent power. Anything shorter (such as "Lord Jesus, have mercy") would feel too "hot." After test-driving different forms of the Prayer, "Lord Jesus Christ, have mercy on me" seemed the best fit for me.

The Jesus Prayer has two parts: you call on the name of the Lord, and then you ask him for mercy. Calling on "the name of the Lord" is a phrase familiar to us from the Scriptures, but if you stop and think about it, why not just call on God? Why include that extra bit about his name?

In the ancient world, a name was not merely a label; it invoked a person's presence and power. In the book of Psalms alone there are nearly thirty references to God's name. This emphasis in the Old Testament is carried over into the New Testament as well, and applied to the name of Christ; when St. Peter prays for a lame man to be healed, he doesn't say, "in Jesus Christ, walk" but "in the *name* of Jesus Christ of Nazareth, walk" (Acts 3:6). In Philippians we read, "At the *name* of Jesus every knee should bow" (Phil. 2:10); not just at the presence of Christ, but at his name.

"The name of Jesus" doesn't mean J-E-S-U-S, however. That was a pretty common name at the time—in Hebrew it's "Joshua," and "Jesus" is how we pronounce the Greek transliteration. It's not those five letters that are powerful, but the *person* of Jesus.

In Irénée Hausherr's fascinating book, *The Name of Jesus*, I learned that the early Christians did not call their Lord by the name "Jesus" alone, as is often done in contemporary hymns and prayers. Anyone, even a nonbeliever, could call this person "Jesus." What gave evidence of Christian faith was to call him "Jesus Christ," making the claim that he is the Messiah of Israel, come to fulfill God's plan in human history. (*Messiah* in Hebrew and *Christ* in Greek both mean "anointed one.") Christians would also call him "Lord," proclaiming that this Jesus is their master and they seek to do his will. As St. Paul said, "No one can say 'Jesus is Lord' except by the Holy Spirit" (1 Cor. 12:3).

So, calling on "the name of Jesus" meant more than saying the word *Jesus*; it meant invoking his whole person as he is revealed in glory, the eternal Messiah and the Lord of your life. When you say, "Lord Jesus Christ," you have already begun to pray.

In saying the Jesus Prayer, we're not trying to get down to the shortest form possible, or to say only the name "Jesus" over and over again. (It's not the same as one-word Centering Prayer, developed by Trappist monks in the 1970s.) Though our world has become reflexively informal, there is something to be said for awarding our God and King the titles that he alone deserves. (I recall the scholar who, discomfited with the trend toward calling St. Paul merely "Paul," asked, "Couldn't we at least call him 'Mr. Paul'?")

This emphasis on the name of Jesus continued after the time of the New Testament. A work written around AD 125, *The Shepherd of Hermas*, states that the name of Jesus "upholds the entire world." About a hundred years later, the theologian Origen (AD 185–254) wrote, "Even today the name of Jesus heals the sick and drives out devils."

But Origen goes on to say something else about Jesus' name. He says that it "infuses a wonderful meekness and tranquility of character, love for mankind, and kindness and gentleness." It seems that Origen is talking about meditating on the name of Jesus, repeating it and cherishing it, and that this transforms a believer's character. This appears to be the earliest reference to prayerful repetition of the name of Jesus.

As I say the Prayer, I find that different parts of it "light up" for me, just as the Lord's Prayer reveals different facets as I pray it, from one day and one year to the next. I once asked Fr. George, my spiritual father at that time, if it would be all right for me to say the first and second phrases of the Jesus Prayer with two different emphases, thinking of Christ's divinity and majesty as I say "Lord Jesus Christ," and his compassion with "have mercy on me." But

Fr. George said that I should not do that, and should intend the Prayer as one single thought. I think this comes naturally when you are fully aware of the presence of the Lord whom you are addressing. When you say, "I love you," to your beloved, it is a single, fully integrated idea, going forth with all the energy of your body and mind; you are not reflecting on the various interpretations of *love*.

A similar idea appears in *The Ladder of Divine Ascent* by St. John Climacus, abbot of the monastery on Mt. Sinai (AD 525–606; *klimakos* is Greek for "ladder"). He advises that a monk use the Jesus Prayer when going to sleep and when getting up, and describes it as *monologistos*, that is, "one-worded": the Prayer comprises a single idea. (By the way, St. John Climacus is the first person to use the term *Jesus Prayer*.)

It's good, basic advice to settle on one form of the Prayer and stick with it. St. Gregory of Sinai (AD 1265–1346) advised monks to begin their prayer by saying, "Lord Jesus Christ, have mercy upon me!" continually, "until you are tired," he says. Then they were to switch to the "second half" of the Prayer and pray, "Jesus, Son of God, have mercy on me," again for many repetitions; when once again weary, they should return to the original form of the Prayer. But, St. Gregory warns, they should not "through laziness" alternate the forms of the Prayer too often. "For, just as plants do not take root if transplanted too frequently, neither do the movements of prayer in the heart if the words are changed frequently."

St. Gregory is envisioning monks who will be praying for hours at a time, which is not likely to be our situation.

But, to this extent, St. Gregory's advice applies to us as well: settle on a form of the Prayer that is best for you and stick with it, so that the habit can take root and not wither due to too much alteration.

Q: *I'M STILL NOT VERY COMFORTABLE WITH ALL THIS BEGGING FOR MERCY.*

People newly introduced to the Jesus Prayer often think: Why should we continually beg God for mercy? Can't we be certain that he has already forgiven us? What, do we have to grovel?

The problem, I think, is that we are imagining a prisoner in court, begging the judge for mercy. It is up to the judge whether to kill this man or free him, and she is justifiably angry. His only hope is to squirm and plead, and beg her to be lenient.

Picture instead the man in Jesus' parable (Lk. 10:30–37) who was robbed and beaten on the road to Jericho, then left for dead. His helplessness was so extreme that he was not even able to ask passersby for mercy, and the priest and scribe passed by on the other side of the road. Yet, the Samaritan saw him and had compassion, and rescued him from death.

That's the kind of "mercy" the Jesus Prayer asks for. We are not trying to get off the hook for a crime, but recognizing how the infection of sin has damaged us. Revealing all the extent of our illness to the heavenly physician, we seek his compassionate healing.

The word in Hebrew is *hesed*, which has the sense of long-suffering love. The prophet Hosea married a woman who was a prostitute. Though she betrayed him many times, he kept seeking her and drawing her back again to himself. That is *hesed* love, long-suffering love, a love that is valiant and breaks through the walls of self-love and pride.

In Greek, the word is *eleos*, and many of the Western liturgical churches still pray in Greek, "Kyrie, *eleison*," that is, "Lord, have mercy."

A listener in the ancient church would have heard a resonance between *eleos* and *elaion*, the word for olive oil. Your experience with olive oil might be limited to salads, but in the ancient Mediterranean world, olive oil was used in a wide variety of ways, and filled essential roles. A wick placed in a clay lamp filled with olive oil could burn and illuminate the darkness. Medicinal herbs were combined with olive oil for healing; the Good Samaritan "bound up [the beaten man's] wounds, pouring on oil and wine" (the latter for the antiseptic quality of alcohol). Olive oil would also be a medium for fragrant herbs in the making of perfume. And of course it would be eaten; in a region where there were few sources of fat, olive oil provided essential nutrition. Sufficient fat in the diet conferred a healthy glow, and the psalmist thanks God for giving "wine to gladden the heart of man, and oil to make his face shine" (Ps. 104:15). This poetic echo between *eleos* and *elaion* contributed to a richer sense of "mercy" than we perceive in English.

I would guess that the majority of Christians I talk to don't particularly feel a need for mercy. They might think of repentance as an initial step toward salvation, but that once you have become a follower of Jesus Christ, once you're baptized and going regularly to church, you're set for life. There's still plenty of work to do, of course—work for the poor, for justice, for the church, for your family—but as far as you go, personally, you're pretty much done.

In the contemporary West, repentance is now considered an introductory activity to life in Christ (if it's considered at all); in the East, repentance lasts for a lifetime. Salvation means healing from the sickness of sin, and we are always seeking to confront the sin that infects us, and to be healed at ever deeper levels.

Q: HOW FAST SHOULD I SAY THE PRAYER?

As you pray, you must turn away from focusing on other thoughts, and that may influence how rapidly you say it. Most times a "walking pace," andante, is about right. Sometimes, though, you might need to say it very quickly, tying the end of one prayer to the beginning of the next, in order to keep a crack from opening up where other thoughts could push their way in. When I'm agitated or worried, I have to think the words of the silent prayer firmly and "mind the gap" (as the announcement goes in the London subway) so that unwanted thoughts don't sneak through.

On the other hand, sometimes you may feel so absorbed in the Prayer that you are savoring every word and want to pray it very slowly. You may repeat it a single time, and then coast for awhile—like the blissful feeling in childhood of cranking up a bicycle to a good speed, then standing on the pedals and flying.

And I sometimes feel as though I can't repeat the Prayer at all—his glory is so momentous and powerful. I just keep looking at the Prayer in my mind, with wonder. The Prayer is a medium of communication, very likely two-way communication, so the texture of it can vary as earthly conversations do.

I'm talking about the dedicated prayer time, when I'm doing nothing else but praying. The rest of the time, I get the Prayer going whenever I think of it. But if the test is repeating the Jesus Prayer all the time, I am nowhere near that. Over and over, every day, I notice that I'm not praying.

So I was encouraged to read this passage, taken from a letter that St. Theophan the Recluse (AD 1815–94) wrote to one of his spiritual children: "You regret that the Jesus Prayer is not unceasing, that you do not recite it constantly. But constant repetition is not required. What is required is a constant aliveness to God—an aliveness present when you talk, read, watch, or examine something." Constant repetition of the Prayer can lead you to remaining in God's presence, but if you can do that without repeating the Prayer, it is all right.

The main thing is to cultivate profound gratitude to God, which comes naturally the more you see your own sin. Without a fresh, strong, authentic yearning for God, St. Theophan says, "the Prayer is dry food."

Q: BUT WHAT IF I DON'T FEEL AWE— WHAT IF I DON'T FEEL ANYTHING?

We don't have any control over how and when God makes himself known to us. But we do have some say about how we regard him. A few years ago I became aware of something that disturbed me; I realized that when I thought of Jesus, I wasn't thinking of something on the order of God Almighty. When I thought of him, I pictured something about the size of a mayor. I approached him with a degree of respect, but affably, and not as if I was truly convinced that he is the Son of God.

This worried me. It was all well and good for me to repeat the Nicene Creed each day, and to say that I believe Jesus Christ is "Light of Light, True God of True God; begotten, not made; of one essence with the Father," and so forth. I affirm that intellectually, without hesitation. But my actual functioning belief, as I went through the day, appeared to be set at a lower, and rather more insulting, level.

Since then, I've taken care to keep in mind the *immensity* of God. When I pray to him, I am speaking to the Creator of the universe. How negligible I am in comparison! My entire life, every word I've said, every memory I have, would be to him less than the blink of an eye. Yet he loves me more than I love him. Millions and millions before me have prayed to him, and their bodies have disintegrated to dust, as mine will in turn. But he will remain. His reign will never end. "Suddenly the Judge shall come, and the deeds of each will be revealed," an Orthodox prayer says. "But with fear we cry out in the middle of the night: 'Holy, Holy, Holy art thou, O Lord!'"

There was a misguided attempt in the last century to make God more approachable, maybe even more human (as if we don't have enough of that already). But it was a misrepresentation. God really is more immense and majestic than we can begin to conceive. Most of us need a course in remedial awe.

So be aware of this possible flaw, and try to bring your image of God more into line with the reality. This is helpful not just with the Jesus Prayer, but with intercessory and other prayers too. If I am praying about a strained relationship with someone I care about, I can recall that God is *inside* that person by right as their creator, and he can teach me how to understand and love them the way he does. If I'm worried about money—all money is Monopoly money to God.

St. John of Kronstadt (AD 1829–1908) was a renowned spiritual elder, though not a monk; he was a married parish priest in the Russian seaport of Kronstadt, and very much loved for his kindness. He wrote:

> When you pray, represent God alone before you, God in Trinity, and none other beside him. Represent to yourself that God is in the world as the soul is in the body, though he is infinitely greater than the world, and is not limited by it. Your body is small, and it is wholly penetrated by your finite soul; the world is large, but God is infinitely great, and fills the whole creation.

It's strange how comfortably we tolerate self-delusion in this regard. If I went around thinking that dark is light or wet is dry, well, that would be alarming. But I can habitually think of Jesus as a minor official, and it doesn't cause much concern. If I'm going to hope for any transforming benefit from prayer, I must begin by at least holding fast to reality.

If reverence is missing, the Jesus Prayer could possibly backfire, numbing you to the presence of God. St. Theophan wrote:

> With regard to spiritual prayer, take one precaution. Beware lest in ceaselessly remembering God you forget also to kindle fear, and awe, and the desire to fall down as dust before the face of God—our most merciful Father, but also our dread Judge. Frequent recollection of God without reverence blunts the feeling of the fear of God, and thereby deprives us of the saving influence that this sense of fear—and it alone—can produce in our spiritual life.

Q: BUT HAVEN'T WE PROGRESSED BEYOND FEAR OF GOD? IT SOUNDS SO NEGATIVE.

Yet for Christians throughout history, fear of God was something they both valued and sought. It seems that they understood something we don't. Saints through the ages have always prayed for deeper repentance, though they would have looked holy enough to us. I think they perceived that, the more you have a "broken and contrite heart"

(Ps. 51:17), the better you can sense the Lord's presence. There is a way that the two fit together, or even function together: the more you know yourself in penitence, the more you know God in his compassion.

Through the centuries, spiritual giants have sought "true repentance." Spiritual elders have always urged their children to cultivate holy fear and compunction, and to pray to receive those traits if they didn't come naturally.

There's no question that such talk seems strange to us today. But there's nothing that really fills its place. I think this results in a certain aimlessness in church life, as if we're marking time, yet sense that something we can't quite identify is missing. It's not for any lack of positive activity; pastors and church leaders work hard to provide a wide range of content-rich programs and ministries. Most churches provide opportunities to be active in one context or another nearly around the clock. But even in the midst of that busyness it can still seem like nothing is quite hitting the center of the target. What is the Christian life for, anyway? Are we just supposed to keep ourselves constructively occupied till it's time to go home?

People who sense that what they're missing is a spiritual dimension find that there are many varieties of spirituality available to choose from. But if the classic emphasis on penitence has been removed, those disciplines won't work for us the same way they did for the centuries of holy men and women before us.

For example, many who begin to practice a prayer discipline (whether the Jesus Prayer or something else) experience transitory sensations of warmth or sweetness in the region of the heart. St. Theophan the Recluse wrote to one of his spiritual children that this is not unusual, because "sweetness goes of necessity with true service." As steadfastness in prayer increases, the concentration of attention within generates a pleasantly warm and sweet sensation. But this is a natural, and perhaps even physical, effect (more on that later); it's not what we should be seeking. St. Theophan wrote:

> The most important thing in prayer is to stand before God in reverence and fear, with the mind in the heart, for this sobers and disperses every folly and plants contrition before God in the heart. These feelings of fear and sorrow in the sight of God, the broken and contrite heart, are the principal features of true inner prayer, and the test of every prayer, by which we can tell whether or not our prayer is performed as it should be. If they are present, prayer is in order. When they are absent, prayer is not in its true course and must be brought back to its proper condition.

> If we lack this sense of sorrow and contrition, then sweetness and warmth may breed self-conceit; and that is spiritual pride, and will lead to pernicious illusion. Then the sweetness and warmth will vanish, leaving only their memory, but the soul will imagine that it has them. Of this you should be afraid, and so you must increasingly kindle in your heart the fear of God, lowliness, contrite prostration before him, walking always in his presence.

The Jesus Prayer is in harmony with all classic forms of Christian devotion in emphasizing repentance, reverence, and fear of God. Some people understand that readily and find it invigorating. I'm one of them, but I also find it far from straightforward to practice, since my clever ego finds a million ways to deceive me. I think it would be even harder to practice this more challenging form of Christianity if I weren't surrounded by family, friends, and fellow worshipers who understand it too, and support me. There's probably a spiritual variation on Gresham's law, "Bad money drives out good," along the lines of, "Undemanding Christianity undermines challenging Christianity."

But others find this emphasis on penitence strange and off-putting. To those I would say: keep an open mind. What seems to be a bad fit to you may be the very thing that will transform you. After all, if you pick and choose from the spiritual treasury whatever seems most appealing, your highest authority is your own opinion—your personal tastes and preferences. And those are self-reinforcing; your personal inclinations will go right on conforming you to the way you already are.

You cannot choose the thing that will change you. The thing that will change you may well look strange from the outside. My advice is to accept the ancient spiritual disciplines as a complete, integrated healing program, rather than picking and choosing to fit. Some kind of wisdom has been worked out in them over the centuries. This net wisdom may well be smarter than you are, because your experience is limited, and also conditioned by your surrounding culture. Though you think you know yourself and your needs better than anyone, you likely have blind spots; we all do. The advice to continue seeking repentance is so consistent throughout Christian spirituality that I think it's worth taking seriously.

You're free to practice this Prayer (or any other prayer) however you want, of course. But if you tinker with it, at some point it is no longer the classic Jesus Prayer. It has turned into a new prayer discipline, and even if it has numerous beautiful elements, you tailored it to fit your preferences. How transformative can that be?

On the other hand, authentic transformation has a cost. Profound change is bound to be unsettling, and not as congenial as being a self-made "spiritual" person. I like to say, "Everyone wants to be transformed, but nobody wants to change."

Q: WHAT GOOD IS REPENTANCE, THOUGH? WHAT'S THE POINT?

Salvation means healing from the sickness of sin, so we are always seeking to confront the sin that infects us, and be healed at ever deeper levels. We spoke earlier about having a sense of urgency in our spiritual lives, and this is the root of that urgency. The lingering presence of sin damages our ability to see reality clearly. It darkens the nous. Sin also strengthens the power of the evil one, and helps him spread suffering and injustice in the world. No wonder we yearn for everything that is bent or damaged in us to be burned away by the radiance of Christ.

Only Christ the Physician can know how the healing should progress, how quickly things should be dealt with, or in what order. Nothing found there will be surprising to him, because he sees all the way through us already. So it is pointless to make excuses, to shift blame or try to cover up. He knows far worse about us than we could stand to know about ourselves. Yet he loves us completely, loves us more than anyone in the world could ever love us. This combination, of being utterly known, yet unconditionally loved, is the only true liberation. The truth really does set us free.

You may feel aware of one particular sin that "clings so closely" (Heb. 12:1), a sin that embarrasses or frightens you. You feel certain that it has to be the first to go, and so devote to it all your fretful attention. You may have made vehement vows to never fall again, and yet have fallen numerous times. Such patterns potentially lead to despair, in which a person simply gives up hope of salvation, and stops trying. This state is called *acedia* (pronounced "ack-eed-THEE-ah"). In the list of Seven Deadly Sins it appears under the name Sloth (though that's not a good synonym, actually).

But the Lord may know something about the underlying structure of your sin that you don't. It may be that some other debility, maybe something you're not even aware of, is holding that big sin in place, and that has to be dealt with first. You might think that the Lord cannot stand the presence of your ugly sin, but he has been standing it a long time already, and he's not going to stop loving you now. If he can be patient enough to bring about a healing that is permanent, you can too; all you have to do is let him love you.

The stance of continuing repentance is a delicate balance: we take full responsibility for our participation in the world's fog of sin, while also knowing we are helpless to stop; we recognize that our sin empowers the evil one and contributes to the world's suffering, yet recognize that his defeat is guaranteed and our Lord will reign forever. Placing all our trust in Christ, we continually cry out for mercy.

The urgency of our request for mercy is not because we think the Lord might forget to help us, or might not be able; we know that he is all-love and all-powerful. The urgency is due instead to skepticism about *ourselves*. We know how treacherous our hearts can be. The Lord said, "He who endures to the end will be saved" (Mt. 10:22), but how do we know that we will endure to the end? Is there some temptation that we finally would not resist, something that might pull us away from the kingdom? We ask for mercy in this as well, that we be preserved in the faith and brought safely to the end.

There have been so many times I've thought about the Lord, and felt my heart lift, and said to him, "Lord, I love you." And then I think about how inconstant my heart is, how flimsy my love, how selfish and self-defensive I am; in a choice between my comfort and safety on one hand, and our Lord on the other, I might well have a hard time deciding. So after I say, "Lord, I love you," I say, "But maybe I don't, really. You know whether I love you or not. I don't know, but you know." For these and many other reasons, we ask again and again for mercy.

Q: *IS IT RIGHT TO ASK OVER AND OVER FOR ANYTHING? DIDN'T JESUS SAY SOMETHING ABOUT "VAIN REPETITION"?*

In the King James Version of the Bible, Jesus warns, "Use not vain repetitions, as the heathen do" (Mt. 6:7), and some people worry that the Jesus Prayer falls into that category. So we have to ask, what was Jesus referring to? How *did* the heathen use vain repetitions? Jesus continues, "for they think that they shall be heard for their much speaking." It sounds like he's talking about a pagan practice of piling up elaborate language and fancy compliments in order to get the gods to listen.

Then Jesus says, "Pray then like this: Our Father who art in heaven. . . ." He invites us to pray in a simple, direct style. And apparently it's all right to repeat the Lord's Prayer; you don't have to make up entirely new words every time you begin to pray.

So it's not repetition that's the problem; it's *vain* repetition, the kind of thing those pagans were doing, using empty phrases and false compliments. But if a prayer is sincere, it's never in vain.

You can think about repetition this way. Imagine a couple of newlyweds on their honeymoon. At a tender moment, the husband says, "I love you, I love you, I love you." Will the bride say, "I heard you the first time"?

It's not technically *necessary* to repeat "I love you," as if repetition would add to or change the message. If you could stretch it out and say it slowly enough, you could, in theory, make one "I love you" last a whole life long. But, because we live in time, when we get to the end we have to go back to the beginning.

It's the same with the Jesus Prayer. If we're going to pray it constantly, we'll have to keep starting over. I think you'll find that, as with "I love you," as you repeat the Jesus Prayer over the years its meaning gets deeper and deeper.

Q: *SO THE CONTENT OF THE PRAYER SEEMS TO CHANGE AS YOU SAY IT, OVER THE YEARS?*

Yes. There is a succession of stages: first, of saying the Prayer solely with your will, then saying it with your whole mind and inner awareness, and then saying it with that awareness rooted in the heart. After that, the Prayer may become self-activating.

All along the way you will be growing more and more adept at silencing your inner chatter and tuning in to God; this whole process is a matter of perception training, as you might train your palate to differentiate among varieties of wine. God is already at work within you right now in many ways you don't perceive; with practice, you can learn to hear and see and cooperate with that work—not just within yourself, but also in the world.

Metropolitan Kallistos Ware writes, "To pray is to pass from the state where grace is present in our hearts secretly and unconsciously, to the point of full inner perception and conscious awareness when we experience and *feel* the activity of the Spirit directly." (Not feeling with your emotions, but by direct perception—as you'd say that you felt a rain-drop hit your skin.)

The way this encounter feels within us will change over time. When a man and woman meet and begin falling in love, the thrilling thing is how *different* each seems to the other. There is always some new thing to learn about this fascinating and wholly original person. They're called "the opposite sex" for a reason. Every element that suggests a contrast—his muscles, her softness—is exciting and savory.

Over time, however, love increasingly is shaped by shared experience. The two go forward side-by-side, and time-tested love grows deeper. They even come to look alike, and share common gestures and facial expressions. The superficial thrill of differentness is great for forging the initial link between two people, but that phase is supposed to pass into one of deeper loyalty and commitment, and ever-deepening communion.

(Sadly, this is getting to be lost wisdom. Popular entertainment virtually always focuses on the initial falling in love, and when a couple begins to make the natural shift to a quieter, deeper, assimilative union, they may mistakenly think that love has died. C.S. Lewis said something perceptive about the thrill of taking up a new spirituality being like diving into a pool. Once you're in the water, you're supposed to start swimming; if you keep climbing out to dive in again, you're missing the point. The same could be said about a culture in which people are unfairly deceived into thinking that the initial thrill is all there is to love.)

A new couple has much to talk about, but an old couple can share a deep unity without saying a word, sitting side by side before the fire. Likewise, initial experience with the Lord may be extraordinarily lively, because you are so *different* from him. Years pass, and by his grace, you grow more like him, become more conformed to his "likeness" (Gen. 1:26); communion with him grows more familiar, and for that reason, more profound.

So, while there may be exciting spiritual sensations at the beginning of the journey, as these fade something deeper and stronger will emerge. The goal is to hear that quiet voice always, guiding every thought and every step. "Your ears shall hear a word behind you, saying, 'This is the way, walk in it' when you turn to the right or when you turn to the left" (Isa. 30:21).

Q: WHAT DOES IT MEAN TO HAVE THE AWARENESS ROOTED IN THE HEART? WHAT IS THE HEART, ANYWAY?

As we saw earlier, in the Scriptures, thinking is done in the heart rather than the head. The phrase "thoughts of the heart" recurs throughout both Testaments. But the heart is more than the source of thoughts and emotions. In Scripture, the heart is understood as the center of a person's entire being. It is "home base." Your heart governs your body, but also every aspect of your consciousness, your thoughts (good and bad), your plans, fears, memories, emotions. The Lord says, "My son, give me your heart" (Prov. 23:26).

Just as we find the pattern of the cosmos replicated inside a cell, all of Creation is present within your heart. The desert monk St. Macarius wrote, "The heart itself is but a small vessel, yet dragons are there, and there also are lions; there are poisonous beasts and all the treasures of evil. There also are rough and uneven roads; there are precipices. But there too is God; the angels, the life, and the kingdom; the light and the apostles, the heavenly cities and the treasures of grace—all things are there." That is how the *hesychast* elders understood Jesus' saying, "The Kingdom of God is within you" (Lk. 17:21).

(In some English translations that reads, "The Kingdom of God is in the midst of you," but elsewhere in the Bible the preposition *entos* means the inside of something, so I think that is the meaning here as well. For example, Jesus told the Pharisees that they clean only the outside of the cup, "but *entos* you are full of extortion and wickedness" (Lk 11:39). Psalm 103 begins, "Bless the Lord, O my soul, and all that is *entos* me, bless his holy name!")

As we noted earlier, practicing the Jesus Prayer can develop into "prayer of the heart." St. Nicodemus of the Holy Mountain (AD 1749–1809), one of editors of the *Philokalia*, wrote: "Prayer of the heart . . . consists principally of a person placing his mind within the heart and, without speaking with his mouth, but only with inner words spoken in the heart, saying this brief and single prayer: 'Lord Jesus Christ, Son of God, have mercy on me.'"

So the work of the Jesus Prayer is to train the perceptive mind, the nous, to enter and dwell in the heart; to "bring the nous down into the heart" as it is phrased, and attend to the presence of God there, and tune in to his voice.

Q: *I DON'T GET IT. YOU CAN TRANSPORT YOUR MIND AROUND TO DIFFERENT PARTS OF YOUR BODY?*

This initially sounds so absurd that you think, "This must have some metaphoric meaning." But it's more literal than you'd think. The reason it sounds strange is because we still reflexively think of mind and body as separate entities. That's a fallacy—a popular fallacy, one that we encounter practically from birth, but absent from the Bible as well as from Jewish and early Christian theology. The aware and living part of you permeates your entire body, and when body and soul are separated at death it is an unnatural rending. Just as Creation "waits with eager longing for the revealing of the sons of God" (Rom. 8:19), when all Creation will be fully restored, your soul and body will be yearning for their reunion at the end of time.

We see in the Scriptures that God's presence can permeate our physical being just as it can our souls. When Moses came down from Mt. Sinai carrying the tablets of the Law, "the skin of his face shone because he had been talking with God" (Ex. 34:29). "God is light" (1 Jn.1:5), and it appears that God's light can be absorbed by matter, including a human body, so that a person's face could glow.

At his Transfiguration, Christ's "face shone like the sun" (Mt. 17:2). This is our destiny, too. St. John was present at the Transfiguration, and writes, "It does not yet appear what we shall be, but we know that when he appears we shall be like him, for we shall see him as he is" (1 Jn. 3:2). St. Paul suggests that Moses veiled his face so that the people would not "see the end of the fading splendor"

(2 Cor. 3:13). The law he brought was a "dispensation of death," St. Paul says, yet even it was accompanied with visible glory (albeit temporary). "Will not the dispensation of the Spirit be attended with greater splendor? . . . Since we have such a hope, we are very bold. . . . And we all, with unveiled face, beholding the glory of the Lord, are being changed into his likeness from one degree of glory to another" (2 Cor. 3:7, 8, 12, 18).

It's interesting that, at the Transfiguration, not just Christ's face shone but even "his garments became white as light." So not just human skin, but any kind of matter, such as clothing, could bear this ineffable divine light that conveys the presence of God. This is called, in the East, the "Uncreated Light," to distinguish it from the ordinary, created light of this world. The Uncreated Light is an "energy" of God, a manifestation of his presence. Encounters with the Uncreated Light recur with some frequency in the stories of the saints of the Christian East, and they continue to take place. (If you haven't looked up St. Seraphim of Sarov and Motovilov yet, now's the time.)

I don't want to write much about the Uncreated Light because it can't be explained very well outside an Orthodox context, and because it is wholly outside my experience. (I got a good laugh out of an e-mail that asked, "Have you seen the Uncreated Light? If so, would you please write about it?") But it should not be omitted entirely, since it is bound up with our ultimate destiny; the vision of the Uncreated Light is an attribute of theosis.

Sometimes this light is glimpsed in the course of the journey, too. My spiritual father, Fr. George Calciu, saw it several times. The first time occurred when he was a child of eight, looking at a field of wheat (he was raised in a peasant family in Romania) and thinking of God as Creator. Suddenly the field was full of "Light [that] had no shadow and no perspective. . . . I was as if petrified."

Fr. George was a bold preacher in Communist Romania, and was imprisoned for twenty-one years. In one prison he had been assigned two cellmates with orders to kill him, because he was becoming known in the West as a political prisoner. But he instead converted them to faith in Christ, and one day they were offering a worship service together, Fr. George acting as priest. As he turned to look at them kneeling in prayer, "they were in this Light, visible Light, Uncreated Light but visible. . . . the whole cell was full of Light."

Jesus said, "If your eye is sound, your whole body will be full of light" (Mt. 6:22). The ancient Greeks believed that vision occurred by means of rays or emanations that came out of the eye. Jesus is saying the opposite, and it is more biologically accurate: light comes into the eye, carrying the image with it. Christ speaks of an eye that is "sound," and in Greek, the adjective *haplous* means "healthy" when refer-ring to the eye, and elsewhere means "sincere," "innocent," "simple," or "generous." The contrast of a healthy eye (with reverberations of innocence and simplicity), like a healthy nous, stands against the eye that is not sound, and by which the body is filled with darkness. It's interesting that Jesus makes a point of saying "your whole body" will be full of light or darkness—not just that "you" will be. In Christ our bodies can be full of light, radiant, as the face of Moses at Mt. Sinai.

It's worth taking time to go over this point again, because otherwise we think of prayer as something that goes on, ethereally, somewhere in our vicinity, but that our bodies are fairly irrelevant. Today we are so used to dealing with disembodied personalities, over the phone, over the Internet, that we don't pick up on information that could be communicated physically. When I read nineteenth-century novels, I'm struck by how much time the author devotes to describing the facial features and bearing of the characters, every detail about the set of the jaw and tilt of the eyebrows. There used to be a common language about what particular physical attributes reveal about a person's character, but it has been lost. Our bodies mean more than we think. The practice of the Jesus Prayer incorporates some ancient awareness of the body's role in prayer, a premodern understanding that can help us with reintegration.

Q: *WHAT ABOUT MOVING THE NOUS DOWN TO THE HEART—WHAT IN THE WORLD DOES THAT MEAN?*

I find that it's not too hard to sense "awareness" moving around in the body; if I hit my thumb with a hammer, my whole attention zooms to that spot. If you know what I mean by that, let's take it as a starting point.

In the usual course of things, going through the day, my awareness is usually buzzing around at the top of my head—even above my head, it feels like, if I'm particularly stressed. There is an ungovernable array of thoughts zooming around up there—random, unrelated, generated by all the myriad impressions that greet the senses.

This is exactly the condition the Jesus Prayer aims to repair. Even now I begin to see that if I stop the pointless buzzing and turn to Christ, I can feel my mind coming in for a landing. My thinking becomes less frantic. In comparison, I see how incomplete and inefficient it usually is, jumping from one topic to the next without resolution. The evil one prefers this, to keep me ineffective and scattered. But in the Jesus Prayer there is a relaxed, alert sort of peace, quietly observant.

If you can picture that random "buzzing" near your scalp, let's go on to picture other modes of thinking. (I'm following here a pattern described by Metropolitan Anthony Bloom.) If you have a hard problem to figure out, you "put on your thinking cap." Now your attention is more securely settled inside your head; things are not as drafty. I expect if I asked you to point to the location inside where you solve hard problems, you would point to your forehead. You can almost feel tension build up in a knot there, and you wind up with a headache.

Now imagine that you have just seen a movie with friends, and it affected all of you powerfully, but you came away with different opinions. You're sitting at a café discussing it, and you listen and then put forth your opinion. Now thinking feels easier, doesn't it? It's more fluid. The words aren't as abstract, but are enriched by the images you've seen and by the stimulation of the conversation and your friends' presence. It doesn't seem like the thinking is crammed behind your forehead any more.

But where did it go? My hunch is that the activity seems like a matter of your mouth and larynx. The words are something you savor; you could almost chew them. Conversation with friends doesn't feel, physically, like it's happening in the same place that hard thinking goes on.

For the third level, let's do an experiment. Think about something that is of great importance to you, something about which you have strong convictions—patriotism, the environment, social justice. I think you'll feel a tightening in your chest and at the base of the throat. Even fewer words are necessary now, because the thing you're thinking about is so significant, so rich. It seems that you are not so much thinking in sequential words about an idea, but communing with something inside that engages your whole being, your emotions, thoughts, and very self.

At this point you can get an idea of what it means to say that the Jesus Prayer unifies your inner being. With each of these imagined steps, your inner self became more united and engaged. With each step, the thing you are considering increases in richness, so that fewer words are necessary; each word has pungency.

After this, the next step is to sense this united attention descending further, into the heart. People are usually able to locate these preceding sites or locations of thought after a little reflection, but not the place of the heart; it must be opened by the Holy Spirit. The ancient monastic teachings on the Jesus Prayer included a number of physical components (what posture to adopt, whether to control the pattern of breathing) that were intended to help a beginner make an internal identification of what this site of "the heart" is, so that he would recognize what was happening when that level of prayer commenced. But these elements couldn't cause "prayer of the heart" to take place; that is entirely a gift of grace.

In his lecture on the bodily effects of prayer of the heart, Metropolitan Anthony Bloom said that the heart is "the physical locus of perfect attention" and unites all elements of the self. "Thought concentrated at the heart attains complete cohesion. . . . The whole inner life is 'instantaneanized', i.e., fixed in a permanent present and reduced to unity."

At that point "[i]ntelligence need exert no effort to keep attention from being dispersed. Intelligence plays its true part: it *sees* and *discerns*. . . . Far from clouding and obscuring thought as the emotions do, [this level of prayer] clears it completely. Intelligence remains fully, intensely conscious and free."

This would not be a state of "rapture" or "ecstasy," which in the East is regarded as the experience "not of the perfect, but of novices," according to St. Simeon the New Theologian (AD 949–1022). Spiritual ecstasy discloses limitation: the person is unable to live in the fullness of God "without losing contact with his own fragmentary individual life," says Metropolitan Anthony. The ideal instead is a "perfect union, permanent and unalterable, in which the whole of man is integrated—spirit, soul, and body—without shocks or breaches of equilibrium, in the image of Our Lord Jesus Christ."

When Metropolitan Anthony speaks of this state as being "fixed in a permanent present," he's referring to the way the mind is galvanized, as if by a stroke of lightning, and oriented wholly toward God's presence in the immediate moment, the only moment. He doesn't mean (I think) that the state itself becomes permanent. It is likely to come and go, particularly at first.

Q: DO THOSE FOUR NATURAL LEVELS OF ATTENTION CORRESPOND TO LEVELS OF THE JESUS PRAYER?

Well, to some extent. It's not as if anyone could make a detailed map, because everyone's makeup and history is different. What's more, our omnipotent God is free to do whatever he wants. For that reason I don't much like the schematizing of prayer experience (not even the classic division into three stages of purgation, illumination, and union), because you should remain agile and ready to go along with whatever transpires. Even if an overview could be presented of the "usual" way things progress, you can't know whether you are one of the exceptions. If you think of these descriptions as being like a road map, and that today you are at Charleston and tomorrow you'll get to Fayetteville, you could miss entirely what God intends to do in your particular case. He picked up Philip on the road south of Jerusalem and carried him all the way to Azotus (Acts 8:40).

Still, it can be helpful to get an overview of what others have observed. A recent book titled *Two Elders on the Jesus Prayer* presents an extremely helpful, detailed understanding of the stages of prayer. One of the monks profiled, the beloved Elder Joseph the Hesychast (AD 1898–1959), deserves his own attention; but for the present I'd like to look at the writings of Archbishop Anthony

Golynsky-Mihailovsky (AD 1889–1976). He suffered much under the Communists, says N.M. Novikov, who pieced together the text from scattered notes. Novikov writes: "While in a solitary prison cell his torturers deprived him of sleep for about a year. He learned to sleep while walking, incessantly repeating the Prayer." He was unfailingly kind and forgiving, and "never blamed anyone who had tortured him, indicating that it was through Divine Providence that trials had befallen the country and its people."

In the twenty years after his release, he was a spiritual father to many, and a "soul-reader" (he could understand a person's situation and inner needs without being told). He would give visitors a passage to read from the *Philokalia*, and "visitors would think a little bit and say to themselves, 'But this is about me.' Alternatively, he used to tell an inquirer a 'fictitious' story about somebody's trials, temptations, and life's path. Many years later that man would remember the Archbishop's words and realize that the story was about him."

Abp. Anthony wrote a treatise, "About the Jesus Prayer and the Lord's Grace," intended to help those who want to begin saying the Jesus Prayer. It was circulated underground in handwritten form during his life, and published legally only after the fall of the Soviet Union. In this text he explained that the spiritual fathers who wrote the works gathered in the *Philokalia* had *intentionally skipped over* the first several levels of the Prayer. (So that explains why it can be so hard to get your bearings in those writings.)

In the time of the great elders, he said, "there were many doers who knew it by experience, and there was no need to describe in detail the early stages because there were many instructors who could explain it." Thus, these authors wrote "laconically and mystically. One who is prepared will understand . . . while the unprepared one will not harm himself."

Abp. Anthony goes on, "Not everyone understands that spiritual prayer starts working in a man only after he approaches the complete fulfillment of the will of God. Up to that point, prayer remains only active." (By "active," he means that the Prayer is still being actively repeated by mental effort, and is not yet spontaneously offered by the Holy Spirit.) "He who takes active prayer for spiritual is bitterly mistaken. If the still unfinished act of the carnal mind is taken for spiritual, then this is demonic delusion and tragic loss."

Abp. Anthony goes on to explain why he wrote his treatise: because an unguided person who attempts the Prayer can be beset with doubts as to whether he is doing things right, and can get discouraged and quit, or even blaspheme the work. "This loss dooms a man to immersion in the same mental darkness in which humankind had existed prior to the coming of Christ. . . . I strongly desire for the wise glorification of the Lord to continue, so that the number of those who prepare their hearts as a dwelling for the Lord will increase, and not decrease. . . . I give an account of everything that I myself greatly needed at one point, when I thirsted for virtually every word that is written here now."

Abp. Anthony describes first the beginner's experience, that of saying the Prayer simply as an act of will, a phase variously called "verbal," "vocal," or "oral." He prescribes how many prayers should be said at what times, interspersed with physical gestures. After each ten repetitions, he says, one should make a *metania* (pronounced "meh-TAN-yah"), making the sign of the cross and bowing, reaching the right hand to the floor. After every thirty-three repetitions, one should make three prostrations, kneeling and then touching the forehead to the floor. You don't have to perform those gestures, of course, though you may well benefit if you do. They are a standard part of a monastic's prayer life.

(Prostrations sometimes occur during Orthodox worship services, particularly in Lent. When I was first introduced to this practice I said, "Like the Muslims?" and my friend replied, "The Muslims got it from us." To be more precise, much of the Muslim Middle East used to be Eastern Christian. Christians and Muslims both got the practice from Judaism. A Bible concordance will show many Old Testament references to "They fell on their faces.")

If you are just beginning this work, don't be surprised that it takes intensive mental effort. You will discover over and over that you have continued to repeat the Prayer while your mind wanders. Every single time, bring your mind back. Don't be discouraged, but make it one for one; keep coming back. Gradually, the Prayer becomes not simply easier, but more attractive. The peace at the center, and the beauty of God's presence, begin to attract the mind's attention.

Abp. Anthony notes that this concentration is hard work, so one should get adequate rest to allow the mind to be refreshed and restored. He advises that one try to speak less, express opinions less, and avoid controversy. We can take a cue from that, and try to avoid anything that undermines focused attention. It's well known that we Americans have grown obese on junk food, but we have also become mentally undisciplined through the consuming of junk entertainment. Think about whether the movies and TV shows, video games and websites that you enjoy have the effect of snatching your mind up and carrying it far from reality, like an eagle sending its talons into a mouse. If you feel you are getting nowhere in the Prayer, take a look at what you are doing with the rest of your time, and look for anything that might be exploding your ability to concentrate.

Don't be taken in by any supernatural or visionary experiences. "Any visions, gifts, and revelations, no matter what shape they take, no matter how holy and graceful they appear to you, must be shunned. . . . Man stops perceiving himself as worthy of anything special, because through attention to thoughts and desires he discovers that he is completely buried in sin."

All that would pertain to the beginning stage, Verbal or Oral Prayer. The next stage, according to Abp. Anthony, is Mental Active Prayer. Here the Prayer is still carried on by the action of the mind, rather than effortlessly by the Spirit, but hope begins to awaken as a person can perceive just a bit what the forthcoming fruits can be. The mind "begins immersing itself in prayer gradually and with pleasure. . . . Do not force yourself to move with your attention to the heart—it occurs naturally later."

This stage of the Prayer is marked by a virtually unceasing battle against disruptive thoughts and memories. It's a common saying that the evil one will attack "from the left or from the right." He might present you with disturbing or tempting images, or he might offer you lofty theological thoughts to contemplate. He doesn't mind which, just as long as you stop praying. It is through prayer that God works directly on your soul, and not through theological rumination. So, put away from you all theoretical ideas; say to yourself, "How can you expect to comprehend deep things when you have no control even over your fantasy life?" and turn again to the Prayer. God permits the challenges that will make you stronger; he, not the devil, controls which temptations you confront.

Abp. Anthony says, "Battle is the destiny of a warrior and you must wrestle and not run away from the contest." With every attack, you gain more familiarity with the evil one's tactics, so that his strategies are gradually revealed.

Don't judge anyone. "I am the foremost of sinners," said St. Paul (1 Tim. 1:15). How could that be? You can see people everywhere whose overt sins are more egregious than your own. But you cannot see what they struggle against inside, or know how many or few talents their Master has allotted them to draw on. You can know only yourself, and should expect that the more that knowledge grows, the more you will be shocked at the duplicity and meanness within. Abp. Anthony says, "Even what has been understood up to this point as good turns out to be a cunningly knit web of the devil."

It is common among monastics to note that certain thoughts take up residence and batter away for several days at a time. A monk or nun will be meeting with his or her elder daily, and will air out these besieging thoughts. In giving guidance, the elder will be able to draw on her own personal struggle with sin; it is in being sinners that we are most united, and the availability of such day-by-day guidance is a great blessing. If you have a spiritual mother or father, you may be able to approximate this by communication through e-mail or over the phone. It is by no means necessary that your elder be someone who lives nearby; some of the richest spiritual literature is found in the letters from elders to their spiritual children.

The third level, according to Abp. Anthony, is Mental-Heart Active Prayer, and in it the mind prays within the heart; "the entire inner man prays." The site where attention rests "appears naturally in the depth of the breast, in the region of the heart." It is still "active" because the person still follows her own will sometimes, God's will other times; her whole being has not yet been united in the service of God.

At this point, the heart begins to be immersed in the Prayer (as the mind was, at the first stage), and is warmed by it and attracted to it. Simultaneously, insight into your personal pattern of sin and temptation increases. "A great temple of passions is built in the depth of a self-righteous heart," Abp. Anthony says. Many find that what they had thought of as the most pure and spiritual part of themselves is, in reality, riddled with crafty pride, and worse. He goes on, "This period of time can be the most sorrowful on the entire road of repentance." Monastics may find that the evil one, in desperate fury, manifests as apparitions of terrifying creatures, and even attacks them physically. No such extreme measures will be necessary for most of us, however, because he finds us unresisting to much less strenuous techniques.

The evil one may also "attack from the right" by appearing as an angel of light (2 Cor. 11:14). These temptations are subtle, and those who falter in continuing to pray with attention "receive deep wounds or suffer a complete debacle." As always, the safest road is to remind yourself that no such heavenly manifestation would be visible to someone still as immersed in sin as you are.

The dawning understanding of the extent of disease in the depths of the heart is a shocking realization, but ultimately liberating. The mind joined to the heart can uncover the deep roots of sinful compulsion. The nous's ability to perceive and understand is becoming clearer, and you gain increased strength through these battles. If you are to be a help to others one day, you must have a thorough familiarity with what inner darkness is like, and you carry the textbook in your own heart. Only a thoroughly realistic humility can keep you safe through this turmoil. This humility is born of failure. "Humility is true self-knowledge that is born in the bearing of sorrows amidst failures and powerlessness. That which has been called humility up to this point has been just a prototype of it, some kind of imitation that did not have relation to self-knowledge and was relatively useless."

Abp. Anthony describes a culminating battle with the evil one, terrifying, but one that reveals the devil's ultimate defeat by the power of God. After this, the mind is free to descend fully into the heart. "The Lord Himself, residing in the heart secretly up to this point, starts dwelling openly and with the full authority in this shelter that was destined for Him from the very beginning, and rests there on his throne."

This victory "is where the boundary between the two main periods in the life of the spiritual athlete lies," says Abp. Anthony. He goes on to describe three more levels, all of which are beyond my comprehension. What we've considered so far is plenty for beginners like us. Just focus on keeping your prayer rule faithfully, and eradicating outward and inward sin, including judgmental thoughts about others. Those who are most serious about making progress will want to limit their intake of entertainment, and avoid frivolous conversation and anything else that disrupts the ability to remain in contact with the Lord. The beginners' levels of this prayer may take "years or decades" as Abp. Anthony says, and are more than enough to keep us busy.

Q: *HAVE YOU EXPERIENCED ANY PART OF THIS FIRSTHAND?*

I've experienced some things firsthand, but I don't think I can evaluate them accurately; what happened to me might not be relevant to anyone else, anyway. But I did start getting an awareness of my heart as a locus of prayer about twenty-five years ago. I was at a retreat, attending a casual prayer service, and everyone around me was standing, singing along with the praise hymns and clapping their hands. But I felt a strong need to sit down and be quiet. I had a mental impression of an oil lamp, a red glass votive cup filled with oil that held a floating wick. The wick was burning, but if I became agitated (with sentimental emotion, for example) it would tip and sputter out.

I think that was when I first began to sense the heart. After that, the focus of my prayer began to move inside. I had been praying *out* toward Jesus; he was out there somewhere and I was talking to him. After that experience, I increasingly felt that the "meeting place" where the Lord's presence would appear was on the inside, and not external.

The funny thing was, I don't think I'd ever seen an oil lamp like that. In my Western liturgical tradition, those red glass holders were used to hold a small vigil candle. Now that I'm Orthodox, those oil lamps are everywhere, mostly hanging in front of icons. (Traditionally, they burn olive oil.)

In the following years I intermittently felt very strong, sometimes painful, sensations in my heart. I even went to the doctor to make sure I didn't have a heart disease. These sensations were associated with very strong wordless prayer. When visiting a friend with a Roman Catholic background, I looked at an image she had of Jesus in the likeness known as the Sacred Heart; it shows Jesus' heart exposed, wrapped in thorns, with flames springing from the top. It hit me: "*That's* what it feels like!"

Eventually the sensations of pain and of "movement" (I don't think I can explain that at all) ceased, but the sense of very strong prayer going on inside the heart remained. It was very intermittent. It would just come over me sometimes. I would have had no idea how to approach or cultivate it.

After I became Orthodox and began reading books by Eastern Christian writers, it started to come together. A decisive "click" came when I read a passage by St. Nicephorus the Solitary (d. AD 1339), whose writings are among those collected in the *Philokalia*. "You know that in every person, inner talking is in the breast," he wrote (in response to a monk's question, it seems). "For, when our lips are silent, it is in the breast that we talk and discourse with ourselves, pray and sing psalms, and do other things." (He assumes the reader knows that thinking takes place in the heart, though we don't have a sense of that any more.) "Having banished every thought from this inner talking (for you can do this if you want to), give it the following short prayer: 'Lord Jesus Christ, Son of God, have mercy upon me!'—and force it, instead of all other thought, to have only this one constant cry within."

I knew instantly what he meant by the "talking" part of the heart, and learned to direct my mind to that place for prayer, sometimes finding that prayer was already going on. There are gradations of attention, and this is more or less successful at different times. I am nowhere near doing it "constantly." But I can recognize some of what it entails.

Now, having said all this, I should add that these "heart" experiences I've had may turn out to have nothing at all to do with "prayer of the heart." It's what I've got to go on at the moment, and so I make that connection, but it may one day turn out to have been an erroneous connection, and I'll learn what prayer of the heart *really* means.

There are techniques of breathing and posture taught to monks in order to facilitate recognition of the place of the heart, but Metropolitan Anthony says, "The techniques which facilitate detection and location of this point artificially are [not] designed to produce prayer. . . . Their sole purpose is to teach the *novice*, for whom they are intended, where this optimum center of attention is, so that—when the moment arrives—he may recognize this as his prayer's point of origin and remain there."

It is uncomfortable to talk about the Jesus Prayer in this clinical and technical way. As Elizabeth Behr-Sigel (AD 1907–2005) writes, "A prayer which is technically perfect but which only facilitates personal development, spiritual power and enjoyment, and psychic superiority, is by its very nature a bad prayer."

She adds: "For a believer, Jesus' name is sacred. The commandment not to use the Lord's name in vain must guide our approach to this form of prayer. It would be sacrilegious to try out the Jesus Prayer like . . . going to a new kind of relaxation therapy."

Q: *IT'S HARD NOT TO BE CURIOUS ABOUT WHAT THE TECHNIQUES ARE, THOUGH.*

They're not a secret. In the *Philokalia* and elsewhere, elders describe them to their spiritual children. Regarding breathing, the instruction is to gather your attention together firmly and then follow the intake of breath down to the heart, to the place where it lies in the chest, caressed by the lungs. Understand that this, in itself, does not constitute prayer; it's like "turn left at the corner."

There is also some teaching about keeping the breathing shallow, and even restraining the breath. This may be one of those cases where mind and body influence each other. I've heard that it is impossible to remain angry if you take deep breaths. (I bet I could, though.) In this case, we are trying to focus the attention closely, and when we really concentrate we do tend automatically to "hold our breath." Perhaps it works the other way as well; by holding our breath, we increase control over wandering attention.

Nevertheless, I am told that the breathing technique involves more than this, and cannot be learned from the ancient texts but only conveyed in person. That is why the advice consistently given today is not even to attempt to practice it. You would not be able to work it out by yourself in any case, and might hurt yourself in the process. It's best not to tamper with something as vital and autonomic as respiration. Breathing techniques are certainly not necessary in order to gain the Jesus Prayer.

Those ancient breathing techniques, by the way, are a different matter from forming the habit of saying the Jesus Prayer along with your natural breathing. You might inhale on "Lord Jesus Christ" and exhale on "have mercy on me," or some other variation, whatever feels most natural to you. (My daughter inhales and exhales twice for one repetition of the Prayer.) So don't be concerned that it is dangerous to coordinate the Prayer with your natural breathing. St. John Climacus said, "Let the remembrance of Jesus be united to your breathing."

In my case, however, I first encountered the Jesus Prayer in the classic anonymous memoir from nineteenth-century Russia, *The Way of a Pilgrim*. In that book, the pilgrim describes acquiring the Prayer as a continual habit by associating the words of the Prayer with the beats of his heart. I started trying to do the same thing, and it worked out all right for me. Later I learned that this approach is not encouraged, and in fact, many elders think that it is dangerous and can potentially cause damage to the heart. God protected me, and I advise others to steer clear.

As to posture, the advice is to sit ("on a low stool," says St. Gregory of Sinai), gather your attention, and bring it down into the heart. Then tuck your chin down to your chest ("Press your beard firmly against your chest," says St. Simeon the New Theologian) and, with eyes closed, direct your gaze toward your heart. It is said that, as you continually repeat the Prayer in your heart, the muscles of your neck and shoulders may begin to ache with this unaccustomed strain, as the chin presses down and neck and shoulders roll forward.

St. Gregory Palamas (AD 1296–1359) speaks of this circular posture as helping the nous to circle back into the heart, instead of scattering its attention abroad. He writes, "Outwardly curling himself—so far as is possible—into the form of a circle, in conformity with the mode of action that he tries to establish in his intellect, he also, through this same position of his body, sends into his heart the power of the intellect that is dispersed outwardly when his gaze is turned outward."

Such a position naturally makes it hard to take a deep breath, and I wonder if that is a practical reason for the advice to breathe lightly, mentioned above. I used to be a natural childbirth teacher, and would teach the pregnant women how to take very short, shallow breaths in preparation for labor, for similar reasons; as the muscular womb contracts, it will press up against the diaphragm. There just isn't room for a deep breath.

The rolled-over posture is not necessary, of course, and though I sit down when I say the Jesus Prayer during my mid-night prayers, I don't consciously follow the elders' advice. But here's a strange thing: I find that, on those occasions when the Prayer is particularly strong, I do start leaning forward, curling my upper body, bending my head toward my chest. If I had to say why, I'd say, "I'm trying to get my head as close as possible to my heart." I don't know why that is. Perhaps it has something to do with the electrical impulses of the heart, which extend a short way outside the body; that's how an EKG machine can record heart activity from electrodes placed on the chest. There's content in brain waves—scratch that elbow, write that symphony. Maybe there's content in heart waves as well, and I'm trying to pick up the signal. (I admit I have no idea what I'm talking about. This is what my husband calls "Fred Science.")

Q: *THIS BUSINESS ABOUT GOING FROM THE HEAD TO THE HEART SOUNDS LIKE AN EASTERN RELIGION. ISN'T THERE SOMETHING IN HINDUISM ABOUT DIFFERENT ENERGY LOCATIONS IN THE BODY?*

The Jesus Prayer doesn't have to do with channeling energy, but rather with focusing attention on Christ. But you are right about Hinduism; while there are variations, some common forms of yoga envisage body energy rising up through the body, passing through five or six chakras (energy centers), until reaching the head, where there is divine union. In the Jesus Prayer, concentration, or attention, rather than energy, does not ascend; it descends from the head to the heart.

But the still more salient difference is that the Jesus Prayer is about Jesus. It is not about manipulating energy within the body, or even about having spiritual experiences. It has to do with one who loves you, who is looking you in the eyes. Keep seeking Jesus, and diligently maintain humility. If you aim, instead, at a mystical high, you can fall headlong into self-delusion. This is a real danger, called *plani* by Greeks and *prelest* by Russians.

A further difference between the energy practices in some Eastern religions and the Jesus Prayer is that, in the latter, you should *never* focus your attention on any part of the body below the heart. Other regions, once energized, can stir up impulses and compulsions that will overwhelm you, exaggerating the emotions while dulling the ability to think.

"Ignorant monks, unguided, without experience or discernment," writes Metropolitan Anthony, "have made bitter discovery of what will be introduced into the inner life by concentration of attention upon those zones [below the level of the heart]. . . . Fixation of attention upon any of this zone's centers induces a progressive obscuration of lucid thought and consciousness, ending in their complete eclipse. This gives rise to more or less stable and more or less permanent 'crepuscular states,'" in which the person's ability to think is clouded, while emotions and desires flood the entire being. Instead of Christ's peace, the person knows nothing but "the turbulent fury of irrational desires and appetites," and is overwhelmed. Metropolitan Anthony observes that the end result is often "mental alienation and physiological disorders."

While writing this book I caught a TV broadcast of the 1931 movie *Dr. Jekyll and Mr. Hyde*. That film, an early talkie, wasn't scary because of its primitive special effects, or Mr. Hyde's Neanderthal-like appearance. What made it truly a horror film was how it enabled us to feel Dr. Jekyll's reaction to the emergence of Hyde. Once liberated, that hideous, murderous sadist was liable to emerge spontaneously at any time, endangering everyone Dr. Jekyll loved.

Fredric March won the Oscar for his wrenching performance as Dr. Jekyll. As the extent of his catastrophe became clear, he mourned, "Oh, God. This I did not intend. I saw a light but did not know where it was headed. I have trespassed on your domain. I've gone further than man should go. Forgive me. Help me!" Later, he says resignedly, "I have no soul. I'm beyond the pale. I'm one of the living dead!" As I watched this, I thought it could be an illustration of the misery that befalls one who stirs up the condition Metropolitan Anthony describes.

Q: *BUT DON'T BUDDHIST AND OTHER MEDITATION TECHNIQUES RESULT IN TRANQUILITY AND QUIETING OF THOUGHTS, LIKE THE JESUS PRAYER DOES?*

All over the world, people's bodies work the same, no matter what they believe, so it may be that people everywhere keep discovering the same mechanisms. For example, if taking deep breaths or mentally repeating the same word (no matter what the word is) calms a person down, it would simply be a physiological fact, the way God designed our bodies to work. It shouldn't be surprising that people in different cultures might discover it, just as people around the world eat food and drink water.

The Jesus Prayer has a marvelously unifying effect on a person, clarifying the mental processes, healing memories, bringing all parts of the mental and emotional life into right relation with each other, restoring the body to its healthy role, and uniting every facet of body and soul in vibrant peace. But other meditation techniques make similar claims, and these initial pleasant sensations may be simply physiological. St. Theophan writes to a spiritual child that "concentrated attention in the heart" results in a "feeling of warmth. This is the natural effect. Anyone can achieve it." If that is simply a physical response to quieting and concentrating the attention, then there's no reason it wouldn't occur in other religions or philosophies.

But in Christian prayer there is more. St. Theophan says, "Those who attain the habit of the Jesus Prayer do very well. But if they stop only at this and go no further, they stop half way." He writes:

> The Holy Fathers make a distinction . . . between prayer of the mind in the heart and prayer moved by the Spirit. The first is the conscious action of the praying man, but the second comes *to* a man; and although he is aware of it, it works by itself independently of his efforts. This second kind of prayer, moved by the Spirit, is not something that we can recommend people to practice,

because it does not lie in our power to achieve it. We can desire it, seek it, and receive it gratefully, but we cannot arrive at it whenever we want to.

The Prayer is designed to lead you further into communion with God, and you can prepare for that by practicing the spiritual disciplines, cultivating humility and repentance, and remembering to say the Prayer. "Try to acquire a kind of soreness in your heart," St. Theophan wrote to a spiritual child. "Constant effort will achieve this quickly. There is nothing peculiar in this: the appearance of this pain is a natural effect. It will help you to collect yourself better. But the chief thing is that the Lord, who sees your effort, will give you help and grace in prayer. A different order will then be established in the heart."

On the other hand, he warns, "it is possible . . . to attach our whole attention to this feeling of sweetness and warmth, taking pleasure in it as in a warm room or garment, and to stop at this point, without trying to climb any higher. Some mystics go no further than this, but regard such a state as the highest that man can attain: it immerses them in a kind of nothingness, in a complete suspension of all thought. This is the 'state of contemplation' attained by some mystics." The attainment of tranquility and inner silence is not meant to be the journey's end.

Q: *STILL, ALL THIS REPEATING OF THE SAME WORDS SOUNDS LIKE A MANTRA.*

The Jesus Prayer is not a mantra but an invocation; it is a prayer directed to the one you call "Lord Jesus Christ, Son of God," and whom you ask for mercy. That's not the same thing as calling on the name of another god. The Postal Service will deliver any stamped envelope you put in the mail, but you alone decide what goes in the letter and whose address is on the front.

I don't know a great deal about Buddhism or Hinduism, but it seems all three of our faiths recognize that something is wrong in the world, and things aren't the way they ought to be. We would disagree on what caused this problem and how it is resolved, but we all observe the same prevailing conditions. In all three faiths, death to self-will is recommended as a way of dealing with the pain this situation inflicts.

After that, though, beliefs diverge. The distinctive thing about Christianity, in comparison with Buddhism and Hinduism, is that we don't expect to pursue that renunciation of self-will to the point of losing our sense of personhood and becoming an undifferentiated part of the universe. For Christians, the ultimate reality is interpersonal relationship; personhood is healed and restored, rather than dissolved. There was personhood (of a kind we can't comprehend) before the Creation, among the members of the Trinity. When we draw closer to God, we enter into that ongoing relationship, and become ourselves participants in this eternal love.

Another religion might urge practice of the virtues in order to simplify and lighten relationships with others, so that those connections might gradually be shed. But the way of the Jesus Prayer assumes that, even at the heights of *theosis*, your own distinct personality remains intact, purified and made translucent, serving as a lantern for Christ's light. Even the most advanced spiritual athletes never graduate from caring about other people. Even hermits who have not seen another person for years continue to intercede for specific needs, by the light God gives them, and miraculous stories about this abound. So, there is no spiritual level so high that you escape other people; love is what God is all about. One who is hoping to progress toward theosis will rejoice at the requirements of love, because they constitute spiritual medicine.

There is a saying in the Orthodox Church: "We go to heaven together and to hell alone."

Q: *DOES THIS BUSINESS ABOUT FEELING PRAYER INSIDE THE HEAD OR THE HEART HAVE ANYTHING TO DO WITH THE REPORTS ABOUT "GOD IN THE BRAIN," THE THEORY THAT SPIRITUAL EXPERIENCES ARE JUST ORDINARY, BIOLOGICAL BRAIN EVENTS?*

Some people have used this research to say that spiritual experiences are illusions generated by the brain, and that has never made sense to me. If a woman looks at her daughter, you could record the effect in her brain, along the optic nerve and affecting the limbic center. But that doesn't prove that her daughter isn't there. Science is limited to things it can measure, and something immeasurable, like a mother's love, must be respectfully set to the side. That's frustrating to some scientists, no doubt, but it's hardly accurate to claim that, if you can't measure something, it doesn't exist. However it is accurate to say that everything we consciously experience is *processed* by the brain. That's the brain's job; it's Grand Central Station for intake.

But there's a further complication when it comes to researching the brain effects of religious practice. Scientists can examine the brains of people who are having a self-identified spiritual experience—but all religions don't aim at the same kind of experience. I was puzzled to read of studies showing that when spiritually advanced meditators reach their expected peak, the part of the brain that tracks the body's location and spatial position dims. At that point a sense of being boundariless, "at one with everything," blooms.

When I feel close to God, it's nothing like that. It's almost the opposite. I feel increasingly aware of the presence of another person, another personality, confronting me with love. I feel the delight of (often wordless) communication. It's not a matter of fading into the ethereal "all," but instead a sharpening of awareness, energizing and strong.

A recent issue of *Scientific American Mind* brought these studies together helpfully, and disclosed some interesting divergence among practitioners of different kinds of prayer. Both Buddhist and Christian meditators showed activity in the part of the brain concerned with paying attention. That's encouraging; it's evidence that if you diligently practice keeping your attention on the Prayer and deflecting distractions, you really can get better at it, in a way scientists could observe on a brain scan. Hard work pays off.

But in another area there was a difference between the two groups. Neuroscientist Andrew Newberg tested Buddhists, who sought a "state in which they lose their sense of existence as separate individuals." He found that there was "a large drop in activity in a portion of the parietal lobe," which helps a person keep aware of the position and location of his body. "Because [it] normally aids with navigation and spatial orientation, the neuroscientists surmise that its abnormal silence during meditation underlies the perceived dissolution of physical boundaries and the feeling of being at one with the universe."

However, neuroscientist Mario Beauregard found that when nuns thought about a memory of a powerful experience of God, activity *increased* in the inferior parietal lobe, "paradoxically, the opposite of what Newberg . . . witnessed." This makes sense to me; when I am sensing the presence of God strongly in prayer, I become *more* alert to the present moment, and feel more really *here*.

I think this is the way we react when someone we love comes toward us. The air crackles with energy, the present moment resounds like a musical note, and a profound connection snaps into place between you. It is the opposite of undifferentiated merging into the universe.

The fundamental difference in Christianity is that it is all about love. Love requires two separate persons, who then come into conjunction with each other; the result is a dynamic connection, a charge of energy leaping between them, and that energy is love.

Love is not merely an emotion; it is a force of the universe. Love changes things. Love even changes things at a distance, as prayer experience reveals.

In love, two become one, while never ceasing to be two (or three, in the case of the Trinity, the love that existed before the universe was made). The bottom line is, Christianity is about persons coming together in love. Because of that, it will always be different in its very foundation from a spirituality that looks toward (as the *Scientific American Mind* article puts it) "dissolution of physical boundaries" and loss of a "sense of existence as separate individuals."

Q: *WHAT DID YOU MEAN BY "WHEN THE PRAYER IS PARTICULARLY STRONG"?*

The challenge of the Jesus Prayer, as we've said before, is to keep paying attention. I find in myself so many slight variations of attention that I think I could grade them by percentages. The least attentive would be mere words circling around the top of my head. In my childhood, there was a child-sized train that made laps around the grocery store; sometimes my prayer makes no more progress than that train did, going around and around.

How good God is, though! I didn't know any better when I began saying the Jesus Prayer, but did it in that inattentive way. Nevertheless, it grew, and I gradually gained a sense of how this prayer can work. The saying that "saying the Jesus Prayer will teach you how to say the Jesus Prayer" was true for me. But I know it helps me to be in a faith community where the whole context of the Prayer is practiced, and I don't get any mixed messages as I travel through the week.

Not that I've achieved a profound and stable prayer life. Even today, if I am rushed, I go back to saying the Prayer in an inattentive, superficial way. If I'm alone, I might combat that by saying it out loud. In monasteries, men and women are often started on the Jesus Prayer with an assignment to pray it audibly, so that the ears hear it, and gradually the heart believes it. If you visit a monastery, you may be passed by a monk or nun fulfilling some duty, saying the Jesus Prayer quietly on the way. This is so common among monastics that many works on the Jesus Prayer assume you are in a setting where you will be saying it out loud at first. That is not an indispensable step, but if you have an opportunity to do so when you are alone, you will benefit.

So, one way I might pray is with very little attention, a prayer of little quality, just thinking the words while distracted by other things. This is better than not even thinking the words at all, but not by much.

At a slightly improved level, I could be thinking the words without thinking of anything else, yet looking at the words blankly, externally, without inner engagement. With this sort of attention, the Prayer is going on mechanically, like a tune stuck in your head.

If you started singing along with such a tune, you would engage more of your being, and for me that is the next level. Here I am saying the words inside while thinking about Jesus and directing the Prayer toward him. This is better, but can still be a fairly uncoordinated prayer. It is akin to the kind of intercessory prayer that hammers away without listening. Intercession is much better if it is done with a quality of listening and gazing at a situation, and keeping an open alertness about all the ways the Lord might intervene. More than once I have found that my hammering-type intercessory prayer was actually hammering at the wrong place—as if I had been trying to get a door to open by banging away with all my might, then realized that I was not standing in front of the door at all, but just bruising my knuckles on a stretch of wall.

Further down, I can sense Jesus listening to my prayer. Something similar can happen in an ordinary conversation, that moment when the other person begins to take a deeper interest and tune in to what you're saying. You almost register this physically, as your body relaxes and words come more easily and more honestly. Most of us aren't listened to enough; we are hungry for someone to look in our eyes and listen. This level of the Jesus Prayer is healing and restorative.

A final level, in my limited experience, is one in which I can feel Jesus not just listening but responding. I start sensing feedback, and my attention could be directed this way or that. Everything begins to come together, and my whole being is integrated and strong. I think that some kind of healing goes on, too, below the level of conscious awareness. This level is pretty good!

I'm sure there is much more to come, but that's as far as I can tell you. (And I'm talking only about the varying levels of my ability to pay attention; I'm not taking about stages of the Prayer itself.) It's a mystery why, when prayer can be this good, we still are inclined to avoid it. St. Nicephorus the Solitary writes:

> Force your mind to descend into the heart and to remain there. Accustom it, brother, not to come out of the heart too soon, for at first it feels very lonely in that inner seclusion and imprisonment. But when it gets accustomed to it, it begins on the contrary to dislike its aimless circling outside, for it is no longer unpleasant and wearisome for it to be within. Just as a man who has been away from home, when he returns is beside himself with joy at seeing again his children and wife, embraces them and cannot talk to them enough, so the mind, when it unites with the heart, is filled with unspeakable joy and delight. Then a man sees that the kingdom of heaven is truly within us; and seeing it now in himself, he strives with pure prayer to keep it and strengthen it there.

Q: *HOW CAN YOU KNOW WHETHER THE SPIRIT YOU CAN SENSE LISTENING OR RESPONDING TO YOU IS REALLY JESUS?*

It's good to be cautious about that, particularly if you are not sure whether you have ever sensed this presence. But expect it to be the presence of a *person*, not just a dazzling concept. If you thought you were alone in a room and then became aware that another person was quietly there, you would become alert all over. The presence of another person works on us in a way nothing else does; it instantly marshals many different aspects of awareness, of body as well as mind.

So you should expect that an encounter with God will be an encounter with a person, a personality, an intelligence; and the quality of his presence is simultaneously strong and compassionate.

Also, the Lord's presence is authoritative and instantly commanding. He speaks as one who "has authority" (Mk. 2:10), who is our author, in fact, and knows us better than we know ourselves. Though our sense of our own inner consciousness can be foggy, the presence of God shines through clear and strong. "Even the darkness is not dark to thee" (Ps. 139:12).

By contrast, a deceptive presence, St. Theophan says, "never approaches as an absolute master, but comes as a charmer who seeks acceptance." It comes from the outside, and it doesn't immediately gain your confidence but rather causes you hesitation and doubt. It never has good effects; it never helps you to resist sin or develop humility. One deceived by it will find that "it fires his imagination, encourages the rush of blood, brings him a certain tasteless, poisonous enjoyment, and flatters him insidiously, inspiring him with self-conceit and establishing in his soul an idol—'I.'"

I had an extraordinary inaugural experience with this person, Jesus Christ, when I was twenty-one, and since then I've had a sure and stable sense of who he is. His presence or "personality" is clearly defined and unchanging. At that time (thirty-five years ago, as I write this) I was not a Christian; I was hitchhiking around the British Isles and went into a church in Dublin, strictly as a tourist. While looking at a statue of Jesus, I discovered an "inner radio" had switched on, in my heart, and I could perceive the voice of the Lord, speaking inside me. Since then, it hasn't been difficult for me to tell if it's him, because it has consistently been the same person.

Earlier I said that it irritates me when Christians acquiesce in the notion that experiencing the presence of Christ is the same thing as having an emotional episode focused on Christ. I said that if I say I experienced going to the dentist, then you naturally assume that I really went to the dentist. You don't think I've had an emotional episode that felt just like going to the dentist.

Let's stick with that analogy. Every time I've gone to see my dentist over the years, he's been the same person. Our interaction is different every time, but he and I remain the same people. The other dental patients don't have the same experience I do, because he adapts his professional services to each person's needs—but he's still the same guy. What's more, if a neighbor sees him in the grocery store, or a friend sees him playing tennis in the park, he is *still* the same guy.

In my experience, it's like that with Jesus. He has been the same person over all these years. When I read stories of other people's experiences with Jesus, in other lands, other churches, other centuries, I recognize him there, too. In all the ways that you can recognize a person, even when the context changes, even when the interaction is completely new, I can recognize Jesus my Lord. Everything else can change, but he is the same.

That this living personality has remained so consistent over such a range of continents and centuries would be enough, all by itself, to convince me of the truth of Jesus

Christ. Albert Einstein said, "No one can read the Gospels without feeling the actual presence of Jesus. His personality pulsates in every word. No myth is filled with such life."

Q: CAN SOMEONE FALL INTO DELUSION, EVEN THOUGH TRYING SINCERELY TO PRACTICE THE JESUS PRAYER?

Only if spiritual pride seeps in, so be on guard against it. As we've said before, this can happen if you're looking for mystical experience, or seeking spiritual power or superiority. That's a fertile garden for the evil one to play in. So seek Jesus, not experiences, and expect to continually discover more reasons you should be humble.

I came across this quote the other day, from our friend St. Macarius of Egypt:

> This is the mark of Christianity: however much a man toils, and however many acts of righteousness he performs, to feel that he has done nothing; in fasting to say, "This is not fasting," and in praying, "This is not prayer," and in perseverance at prayer, "I have shown no perseverance; I am only just beginning to practice and to take pains"; and even if he is righteous before God, he should say, "I am not righteous, not I; I do not take pains, but only make a beginning every day."

A radio host once asked me if we can alternate repetitions of the Jesus Prayer with something more "positive" to build up our "self-confidence," since we are, in Christ, "more than conquerors" (Rom. 8:37). Christ is the conqueror, not us, I said, and our self-confidence could do nothing but get in the way. There are plenty of Scriptures warning us not to trust in our own strength.

But humility does seem a strange fit in our culture. My hunch is that this is because the majority of messages directly addressed to us throughout the day come from advertisements, and they rely on the softening power of flattery. It takes some sustained attention and conscious effort to mobilize humility in yourself.

Pride is a slippery thing, but it helps to get a handle on it to note that it has to do with making comparisons; you feel pride when picturing yourself alongside someone else. There are many other kinds of sins that relate only to your needs and desires, but pride arises in the context of relationships. St. Paul wrote, "Do nothing from selfishness or conceit, but in humility count others better than yourselves" (Phil. 2:3).

But pride isn't always about thinking you're *better* than someone else. If you feel less than someone, but stew about it resentfully, that is just another face of pride. Pride can show up as anger, or hurt feelings, or even embarrassment; any twist in a relationship may be rooted in making comparisons, no matter whether that comparison makes you gloat or pout. (By the way, embarrassment is *not* the same thing as repentance.)

St. Paul is an example to us when he says "Christ Jesus came into the world to save sinners. And I am the foremost of sinners" (1 Tim. 1:15). The only person whose inner heart you know is your own, and even that not well, at least not as well as the Lord knows it: "He knew all men and needed no one to bear witness of man; for he himself knew what was in man" (Jn. 2:25). If St. Paul could see himself as the foremost of sinners, maybe you can, too.

We've said before that the way of the Jesus Prayer is concerned with transformation; it's going to change you. But what we haven't said is that it's not going to change you into the kind of person the world looks up to.

There have been times when meekness (that is, strength voluntarily restrained) and humility were valued and admired, but that's not the case now. Look at movie heroes and heroines, and see what the world adores: power, glamour, toughness, witty put-downs, bloody vengeance. The kind of person Christ will make of you is the kind of person our culture does not even *notice*, much less admire.

This is all to our spiritual health, because we get to escape the final twist that is possible in more faithful ages, in which a holy person who has been praised and flattered for her humility falls into the pit, lured by subtle, hidden pride. No, we can be fairly confident that the more gentle and humble we become, the more the world will sneer at us. Thank God for that.

Western Christians who have heard of the Eastern tradition of saints known as "Fools for Christ" may be unaware that this role is usually adopted voluntarily by someone who wants to court the world's contempt. Fools-for-Christ may be perfectly normal psychologically, and may have gifts of beauty or intelligence; but they take on the identity of a madman so that the world will not admire them or think them saintly or wise. Contemporary Christians benefit in this area, too; we don't have to fake madness, because the world already thinks we're crazy.

A good test for humility is whether you are able to love your enemies. This makes sense, because the opposite of pride is humble love, and the most difficult to love are those who hate you. Christ pointed out that everyone loves the people who love them in return; if you love friends and family, you're like everybody else. If you are to show that you are his disciple, you must do more than that.

> Love your enemies and pray for those who persecute you, so that you may be sons of your Father who is in heaven; for he makes his sun rise on the evil and on the good, and sends rain on the just and on the unjust. For if you love those who love you, what reward have you? Do not even the tax collectors do the same? And if you salute only your brethren, what more are you doing than others? Do not even the Gentiles do the same? You, therefore, must be perfect, as your heavenly Father is perfect. (Mt. 5:44–48)

The evil one, of course, is not capable of loving enemies or anyone else, so if you have love toward enemies it is a reassuring sign that you are on the right track. St. Silouan the Athonite (AD 1866–1938) was a widely respected ascetic who lived in a monastery on Mt. Athos. (Thomas Merton called St. Silouan "the most authentic monk of the twentieth century.") St. Silouan taught that love of enemies was the one infallible way to tell that someone is progressing in communion with God and free from delusion. St. Silouan wrote, "The Lord is meek and humble, and loves his creatures. Where the Spirit of the

Lord is, there is humble love for enemies and prayer for the whole world." Even if this is the only virtue you have, in it you have pure gold.

Reading Rachel MacNair's *Perpetration-Induced Traumatic Stress* helped me to develop compassion for enemies. (The author is a Quaker and pacifist, and was for many years president of the antiabortion organization Feminists for Life.) MacNair's book is about the psychological damage people incur from killing or hurting others—whether it's a cop who has to shoot a fleeing criminal, a soldier in wartime, a train engineer who sees someone lying on the tracks but cannot stop in time, or an abortion doctor who spends all day clearing out "the products of conception."

Even trained and supposedly hardened people find it stressful to cause hurt to others. In his article, "The Price of Valor," for the *New Yorker* magazine, Dan Baum found that American soldiers who had lost limbs in Iraq could talk and even joke about their injuries, but when he asked them to talk about the killing they'd done, "a pall would settle over them." A company commander said that it is easier for a soldier to accept the death of a friend than to know that he has shot an enemy. (Of course, there is that 2 percent of people—almost always men—who get an unhealthy kick out of killing, and who perhaps are demonized.)

MacNair tells how the Nazi soldiers who were assigned to shoot prisoners lined up along an open pit were psychologically destroyed by their deeds. Adolf Eichmann observed that "some had committed suicide. Some had gone mad. Most . . . had to rely on alcohol." Their commander said, "Look at the eyes of the men in this Kommando, how deeply shaken they are! These men are finished for the rest of their lives." He himself later succumbed to hallucinations.

Learning about this psychological trauma was touching and, in a way, encouraging to me; it is good to learn that God has placed something inside each of us that recoils in horror from hurting other human beings. We find that even more disturbing than being hurt ourselves. We are created with such an instinctive reverence for human life that the act of shooting those prisoners was profoundly distressing even for those Nazi soldiers. Understanding this makes it easier for me to feel compassion for enemies. We are all made from the same fabric.

Pastor Richard Wurmbrand (whom we met earlier, telling of a priest he met in Romanian Communist prison), wrote of an experience he had while in the prison infirmary, seriously ill with tuberculosis. On his right was a priest named Fr. Iscu, abbot of a monastery, who had been so tortured that he was near death; on Pastor Wurmbrand's left was the Communist officer who had tortured Fr. Iscu. In that volatile climate, a person could be powerful one day and imprisoned the next, and this officer had fallen precipitously out of favor. He had been severely tortured himself, and death was drawing near.

This fallen Communist was in terror as well as pain, and kept asking Pastor Wurmbrand to pray for him. He kept saying, "I can't die, I have committed such terrible crimes."

Fr. Iscu, on the other side, had been listening. After a while he called for two other prisoners to help him. Leaning on them, he slowly and painfully made his way to the officer's bed. He sat on the bedside and reached out to caress the miserable man's head. "I will never forget this gesture," said Pastor Wurmbrand. "I watched a murdered man caressing his murderer!"

Fr. Iscu told the officer, "You are young; you did not know what you were doing. I love you with all my heart." Then he said, "If I who am a sinner can love you so much, imagine Christ, who is Love Incarnate, how much He loves you! And all the Christians whom you have tortured, know that they forgive you, they love you, and Christ loves you. He wishes you to be saved much more than you wish to be saved. You wonder if your sins can be forgiven. He wishes to forgive your sins more than you wish your sins to be forgiven. He desires for you to be with Him in heaven much more than you wish to be in heaven with Him. He is Love. You only need to turn to Him and repent." With that, the officer choked out the words of his confession with tears, and the priest, the one whom he had tortured, spoke the words of God's forgiveness.

Pastor Wurmbrand says that both men died that night. It was Christmas Eve. "But it was not a Christmas Eve in which we simply remembered that two thousand years ago Jesus was born in Bethlehem. It was a Christmas Eve during which Jesus was born in the heart of a Communist murderer."

Q: *BUT I CAN'T FORGIVE MY ENEMY. NOT BECAUSE OF WHAT HAPPENED IN THE PAST; IT'S BECAUSE I'M AFRAID HE'LL DO IT AGAIN.*

I think some people confuse forgiveness with vulnerability. Just because you have forgiven someone, it doesn't mean that you must allow him to go on hurting you. Forgive the past, but make wise decisions about the present and future.

In some situations, you might decide to allow a past enemy to attempt to hurt you, because Christ has so strengthened and healed you that those actions, in fact, no longer hurt. It's possible that permitting and ignoring such attempts to wound you can have a good effect, setting things in motion inside your enemy. The dart that he throws, but has no effect, returns to unsettle him. In this process, something in that enemy's heart may be awakened.

But if her actions still wound you, and she enjoys perceiving that, then permitting it could serve only to confirm her sin. You are never required to allow someone to hurt or abuse you, physically or emotionally, and in a case like that, permitting abuse could make you an enabler and partner in that sin.

Whatever decision you make about your current relationship to that person, as far as the past goes you should simply let it be over and done with. Let go of the desire for vengeance. That's what forgiveness means.

Someone once asked me how we can love an enemy who wishes to kill us and destroy our country. I think for such a one we must grieve as we contemplate his eternal destiny, the weeping in darkness that is the fate of those who reject God. We should pray that the All-Compassionate God will visit such a one and give him an opportunity to know Jesus Christ as Lord. I know this is possible, because God broke in on me when I was a blasphemer and an enemy of Christ. It wouldn't be fair if God did this for me, but not for others. So we should pray for the conversion of our enemies, and love them. We should want all our enemies to come to repentance and knowledge of God's truth, and to see them at the banqueting table one day.

"I tell you, my friends, do not fear those who kill the body, and after that have no more that they can do. But I will warn you whom to fear: fear him who, after he has killed, has power to cast into hell; yes, I tell you, fear him!" (Lk. 12:4–5).

Never gloat over another person's fall. St. Nikolai Velimirovic (AD 1881–1956) wrote:

> He is a man; do not rejoice in his fall. He is your brother; let not your heart leap for joy when he stumbles. God created him for life, and God does not rejoice in his fall. And you also, do not rejoice at that which grieves God. When a man falls, God loses; do you rejoice in the loss of your Creator, of your Parent? When the angels weep, do you rejoice?

> When your enemy falls, pray to God for him, that God will save him; and give thanks to God that you did not fall in the same manner. You are of the same material, both you and he, like two vessels from the hand of the potter. If one vessel breaks, should the

other one smile and rejoice? Behold, the small stone that broke that vessel only waits for someone's hand to raise it to destroy this vessel also. Both vessels are of the same material, and a small stone can destroy a hundred vessels.

When one sheep is lost, should the rest of the flock rejoice? No, they should not. For behold, the shepherd leaves his flock and, being concerned, goes to seek the lost sheep. The shepherd's loss is the flock's loss too. Therefore, do not rejoice when your enemy falls, for your Shepherd and his Shepherd, the Lord Jesus Christ, does not rejoice in his fall.

O Lord Jesus Christ, Thou Good Shepherd, remove malicious joy from our hearts, and in its place plant compassion and brotherly love. To Thee be glory and praise forever. Amen.

Love of enemies is the surest evidence that your life in Christ is in sound health and not verging toward pride or delusion. Yes, there are dangerous possibilities in the spiritual realm, and treachery within your own tangled psyche. The Jesus Prayer is like a lamp, illuminating all that shadowy realm, enabling you to recognize and reject everything that separates you from Christ.

Q: *I'M DISCOURAGED. I CAN'T DO THIS AT ALL.
I AM DISTRACTED EVERY MINUTE.*

It can be clarifying to realize that you are being distracted by *thoughts*. The idea is that gradually you will get to recognize these thoughts when they first pop a head over the horizon, and reject them with no further fuss. The nous stands like a sentinel at the entrance to the heart, recognizing the thoughts as they advance and batting them away.

This stance of watchfulness is called *nepsis*, meaning "vigilance," the wakefulness Jesus praised in the five wise virgins (Mt. 25:11–13). The great athletes of prayer are described as "neptic," for their watchfulness. "Watch at all times, praying that you may have strength to escape all these things that will take place, and to stand before the Son of man" (Lk. 21:36).

Our natural capacity for attention has been affected by the presence of the Internet, I think. It gives us the sense that where we are right now, the place where our bodies are situated, is *not real life*. Real life is out there in cyberspace, where celebrities are doing things worth gawking at, where political enemies are saying things worth deriding. The Internet is so vibrant that it puts our ordinary lives in the shade. It feels as though where we are right now is going on backstage. Even while we sleep, the Internet is charging ahead, scintillating and alive; it never stops.

The foggy pseudo-reality woven by all this digital media has an oppressive effect. Not only does it alienate us from physical reality, nature, our bodies, and the people immediately around us, it conditions us for restlessness.

We have a kind of alertness, all right, but instead of being focused it is endlessly scanning. We gain the habit, while doing something, of looking around for something else to do. The mind doesn't feel comfortable settling down on one thing. So we need to differentiate focused, prayerful attention from the kind of restless alertness that has become our habitual mode.

You'll notice that your initial attempts to focus the mind on Christ will be peppered with extraneous competing thoughts. These thoughts might arise from your own mind or memory, or be provoked by something you see or hear. In general, there is a quality of dispersal, and the mind is airy and distracted, rather than focused and attentive. In the early stages of the Prayer there is a virtually incessant back-and-forth of praying with attention and merely repeating the words while the mind is scattered abroad.

The mechanism by which this is healed is that you begin to build up and develop the part of your mind that *watches your mind*. Instead of being helplessly swept off by a memory, a thought, or something you see, you begin to develop a little patch of interior real estate where you can stand beside the Lord and observe all that comes and goes. You begin to perceive patterns in your thinking. You come to see that certain topics or sights are particularly disruptive to your inner peace. With practice, you get better at remaining in this place of steady observation, and are not as easily overthrown. (Of course, to the extent you can, you should avoid those things and people that agitate you. For example, if you know that a war movie is going to stir up your craving for vengeance, don't go see it.)

Over time you will get better at retaining your nous within yourself, where it is resilient and grounded, where it can look with discernment on all that approaches. Train your nous to remain inside the heart, and give up its pointless and debilitating exterior wandering.

Sometimes these thoughts come from hurtful memories or something you happen to see, but sometimes they come from the devil. Remember that his goal is to tempt and distract us, and induce us to doubt God; he doesn't want to stage a scene out of *The Exorcist*, because the more visible he is, the more vulnerable he is. I read recently this interesting point: if the devil is behind phenomena like mediums who contact the dead, it is in his interest *not* to provide conclusive evidence that the medium's messages are authentic. The devil would prefer to keep things uncertain and keep people guessing. Because if he provided undeniable proof of the authenticity of such spiritual contact, and people became convinced that the spiritual realm was real, it wouldn't require much comparison shopping for them to realize that it is much wiser to be on the side that is *fighting* the devil. Thus, it is in the devil's interest to muddy up such phenomena.

He's a tempter, not a showman. If he can get your attention to drift from prayer without your noticing his presence, it meets his goal. So he keeps attempting to distract us from prayer by throwing disruptive, upsetting, or intoxicating thoughts at the nous, like throwing a brick through a window. These upstart thoughts, whatever their origin, are logismoi.

Thoughts about other people are a common example of logismoi, particularly when you are judging them, or fretting about being judged. A contemporary elder said, "When you say to yourself, 'They are thinking about me . . .' know that this is from the devil."

There's a curious line in the second chapter of Luke's Gospel, where the story of Christ's birth is told. In ancient Israel, forty days after the birth of a male child, a woman would go to the temple for a purification ceremony, and her son would be presented to the Lord. St. Luke tells us that the aged prophet Simeon came up to Mary and Joseph and took the baby Jesus in his arms, thanking God for fulfilling his promise that Simeon would live long enough to see the Christ. While holding the child, Simeon delivered the beautiful prayer, "Lord, now let your servant depart in peace."

But next he said a curious thing. At that time, everyone believed the Messiah would be a military genius who would defeat the Roman occupation army and expel it from the land. Simeon said nothing about political liberation. Instead he said to Mary, "Behold, this child is set for the fall and rising of many in Israel, and for a sign that is spoken against (and a sword will pierce through your own soul also), that thoughts out of many hearts may be revealed" (Lk. 2:34–35).

Why did he say the child has come so that "thoughts out of many hearts may be revealed"? That would have nothing to do with defeating the Roman oppressors. The focus has suddenly shifted to the inner life of thought and heart. Simeon's words prepare the way for Jesus' teachings about the importance of the condition of the inner person. "On the day of judgment men will render account for every careless word they utter" (Mt. 12:36) he said, and, "Nothing is covered that will not be revealed, or hidden that will not be known" (Mt. 10:26). Driving out every extraneous and foolish thought, Jesus really does intend to occupy the whole attention of the heart.

It is interesting that when a baby is born, once she gets over the initial burst of crying, she enters what is called the "quiet alert" state. She looks steadily at all around her, and particularly seeks out eye contact. I can't help but think that this sounds like the quality of attention that is the goal of prayer of the heart. When a baby is first born, she has to do many things she'd never done before; breathe in air, feel cold, and wail. But after she's gotten a bit settled, she becomes quietly alert. Maybe that's not a new thing for her to do; maybe she's been doing that for months, ever since she was awake at all.

It might be that life in the womb is akin to the kind of awareness we seek in the Prayer. If so, when struggling as adults to keep our scattered attention pinned to the Jesus Prayer, it's encouraging to think that perhaps we were once very good at this.

So, don't be discouraged. Even if your prayer feels futile and dry, it is still heard. St. John of Kronstadt said, "When you are praying alone, and your spirit is dejected, and you are wearied and oppressed by your loneliness, remember then, as always, that God the Trinity looks upon you with eyes brighter than the sun; also all the angels, your own Guardian Angel, and all the Saints of God. Truly they do; for they are all one in God, and where God is, there are they also. Where the sun is, thither also are directed all its rays. Try to understand what this means."

Q: *BUT HOW CAN YOU FIGHT AGAINST THOUGHTS, OR LOGISMOI?*

Let's think of a logismos as a temptation, a provocation or suggestion. By stages we pass from merely fielding a thought to being chained to compulsive sin. St. James says: "Each person is tempted when he is lured and enticed by his own desire. Then desire when it has conceived gives birth to sin; and sin when it is full-grown brings forth death" (Jms. 1:14–15).

Orthodox elders identify these steps:

1. Provocation

This is when the thought first appears. St. John of Damascus (AD 676–749) wrote, "Provocation is simply a suggestion coming from the enemy, like 'do this' or 'do that,' such as our Lord himself experienced when he heard the word, 'Command that these stones become bread.' . . . It is not within our power to prevent provocations."

That's a relief; *everyone* is subject to receiving these provoking thoughts, and having them is not your fault. I want to stress this, because sometimes people are distraught at the sight of an ugly thought, and think, "How can such a thing come out of my mind?" But it may well not have had its origin in your mind. It can be a thought thrown your way by the evil one, just to see how you would respond. If he can get you to feel fear and disgust, he's won part of the battle. So don't feel guilty for hearing such thoughts; recall that even Christ could not avoid hearing the devil's suggestions.

The wise abbot called by the pseudonym Fr. Maximos, whose teaching is transcribed in Kyriacos Markides' *Mountain of Silence*, says, "When humans are attacked by such logismoi they ought to feel no guilt whatsoever. They are totally innocent and not responsible for these logismoi."

The desert monk St. John the Dwarf (AD 339–405) purified his soul to the point that he no longer felt temptations. His spiritual father told him, "Go, beseech God to stir up warfare, so that you may regain the affliction and humility that you used to have, for it is by warfare that the soul makes progress." When his temptations returned he no longer prayed that they be taken away, but said, "Lord, give me strength for the fight."

Mother Gavrilia (AD 1897–1992) said that even the great saints cannot avoid being attacked by logismoi. But the nous of a saint offers such thoughts no place to make a home. She said it is like when flies buzz into an empty room; finding no food or anything else to attract them, they buzz back out again.

These thoughts are not necessarily *tempting*, by the way, in the sense of being attractive or appealing. They may be odd and random, or disgusting, or terrifying. They may be temptations to self-hatred. Even if these thoughts hold no attraction, they still serve to disrupt your concentration. The right way to handle this sort of thought is to turn away. Don't get agitated about it, or get caught up in forcefully rejecting it. Just turn your attention back to the Prayer. As they say, you can't stop the birds from flying overhead, but you don't have to let them build a nest in your hair.

You may be aware of emotions rather than thoughts; for example, finding yourself uneasy or angry though you don't know why. Emotions are usually attached to something, so try to identify the thoughts that are troubling you. The demons would much rather manipulate you to act on these emotions blindly, so that the world would become a more miserable place, and no one would catch them instigating the thoughts in the first place. So try to dredge up these thoughts to awareness, and ask yourself whether they are legitimate thoughts, and whether you agree with them. Many a thought loses its power when exposed to light. Don't let them slip by in the shadows, hiding from conscious awareness. Catch the rats by the tails.

Some years ago I was praying one night, as usual, when the thought popped into my head: "What if there is no God?" I was frightened by this and began to pray, "Lord, help me! Rescue me!" Then it dawned on me that, if my first reaction to the suggestion that there is no God is to run to God for help, then I don't really doubt that there is a God. In short, this was not my thought. It was a logismos thrown my way at random, just to see what would happen. As you get more practice at noticing your thought patterns, you'll observe your own examples of this.

The common advice is that you should not try to argue with the provoking thought. A prideful person may think she can dispute with demonic temptation, but then ends up mentally tangled and confused. Only the greatest athletes, after long years of purification from self-will, are capable of doing that. So don't engage with the logismos at all; it might turn out to be stickier than you think. Instead, knowing yourself to be a weak child, run to the arms of the all-compassionate Lord.

2. Interaction

This is the stage at which your nous engages with the thought, whether entertaining it or arguing against it. Even if you intend to defeat the thought, the fact is that it is now occupying your attention. It has a foot in the door—and you are looking at a logismos instead of praying. The advice of the Fathers is consistent: cry out for God's help. Do not attempt to defeat it, and do not grapple with it in any way. Wrap your nous in the Jesus Prayer; as St. John Climacus says, "Flog your enemies with the name of Jesus."

St. Hesychios the Priest (ca. AD 800) wrote, "Intellect is invisibly interlocked in battle with intellect, the demonic intellect with our own. So from the depths of the heart we must at each instant call on Christ to drive the demonic intellect away from us and in his compassion give us the victory."

3. Consent

At this point, the nous has become intoxicated with the thought and embraces it. A sign of this stage is that the nous becomes absorbed in gazing at an image or playing out a fantasy. Whether these images give pleasure or arouse fear, in either case the connection of constant prayer has been broken, and the castle wall is breached. St. Mark the Ascetic (ca. AD 450) says, "Once our thoughts are accompanied by images we have already given them our assent; for a provocation does not involve us in guilt so long as it is not accompanied by images." The nous is able to experience God directly, but when you start having images, it's a sign that you have reverted to being one step removed, and you're only talking to yourself.

Fr. Michael Shanbour, pastor of Christ the Savior Orthodox Mission in Spokane Valley, Washington, writes,

> Religions and philosophies have tried in vain to defy nature itself by reducing the practice of spirituality to a purely mental experience. The Christian faith teaches the opposite. It is precisely mental imagery, the realm of fantasy or imagination, which is most dangerous to the spiritual life. Pure prayer and communion with God is not primarily a mental exercise (in the narrow sense of a cognitive process), but rather an experience of God himself, directly to the nous, unrelated to one's own thoughts and imagination. It is by putting aside fantasies and thoughts, the raw material for demonic activity, and clinging to the image of God, both within and without, that we may receive true spiritual revelation. . . . So profound is this human need for the image of God that we are constantly moving toward one of two poles, or ways: Either we recognize the true God and his image in us, or we construct our own god or gods in our own image.

It is at this point, when we consent to an image or fantasy, that we become responsible for sin, even if as yet no action has taken place. Jesus said that one who is angry at another person is guilty of murder, and one who entertains lustful thoughts is guilty of adultery (Mt. 5:28).

Nonetheless, it is still a good thing if the person can resist going through with the temptation. Fr. Maximos recounts a story about St. John Chrysostom (AD 347–407), who was Patriarch of Constantinople. Some Christians in the city interpreted Christ's words quite literally, and said that even thinking about a sin was fully as spiritually wounding as putting it into action. St. John invited this party of hard-liners to dinner, and told them to fast all day so they would have a big appetite. That evening the table was laden with sumptuous food, and all stood for the blessing. But the prayers went on and on, while the delicious fragrance became nearly overwhelming to these hungry guests.

At the end of the blessing, St. John told them they could depart. They protested: But we haven't eaten yet! St. John pointed out that surely they had been experiencing the meal in a vivid way in their minds; wasn't that the same thing as actually eating it?

4. Captivity

Once the person has consented to the thought, the ability to put up any further resistance crumbles. The temptation is put into action, and that deals a wound to the soul such that it will be weaker the next time this logismos comes around.

5. Passion

After giving way repeatedly, the process from initial thought to final action no longer requires a sequence of stages; the mere appearance of the logismos is sufficient to vanquish all resistance. The term *passion*, in this context, means something akin to a compulsion or addiction. In Greek the word is *pathos*, which means "suffering." It shares a root with *passive*, for the person has been overwhelmed and dominated by this sin.

The passions are usually understood in this negative sense in Orthodox writings, but some elders explore the idea that they are, at root, positive impulses that have been disfigured and misdirected. Anger, for example, can be turned into zeal for the battle against sin; lust can be purified into ardent love for God and all humanity. We are designed for holiness, yet fallen; the compassionate Physician wishes his good design to be set right, not annihilated.

This is a spiritual path that is literally therapeutic: it enables healing. In the West we sometimes hear spiritual approaches derided as "merely therapeutic," meaning that they offer comfort and consolation rather than the challenge of holiness in Christ. This is a genuinely therapeutic approach, however, in which true inner healing takes place. The path is sometimes called, in Greek Orthodox writing, "psychotherapy," meaning literally, "the healing of the soul." The all-compassionate Christ rescues us from the grip of death, and day by day we are enabled to be healed.

How does the mind function, when it is no longer troubled by upstart logismoi and distracting images? St. Hesychios the Priest wrote, "A heart that has been completely emptied of mental images gives birth to divine, mysterious intellections that sport within like fish and dolphins in a calm sea. The sea is fanned by a soft wind, the heart's depth by the Holy Spirit. 'And because you are sons, God has sent forth the spirit of his Son into your hearts, crying, "Abba, Father"'" (Gal. 4:6).

Q: *AREN'T VISIONS SOMETIMES THE REAL THING? I DON'T WANT TO OFFEND GOD IF HE'S TRYING TO TELL ME SOMETHING.*

Of course, there *is* such a thing as a genuine vision or word from God. We hear about them frequently when reading the lives of the saints, and we wouldn't know about those experiences if the saint hadn't told someone.

If God is trying to get through to you with some specific message, he will continue drawing your attention. In my experience, he gets you surrounded. You find that the same topic keeps popping up in the oddest ways, like what the person next to you on the bus is talking about; you start to notice what a friend calls "synchronicities." These occurrences have the advantage of being indisputable; you're not wondering if it really happened, as you might with a wavery vision. If something keeps showing up like this, pray about it: stand mentally before God and hold it up in your hands, and turn it and look at it from all angles. Ask yourself whether you have a sense of it fitting, or not fitting, with his presence. Is there a part of it that seems to mesh, while another part did not?

But if it is more like a hallucination—if some visible or audible thing persists in coming to you in prayer—treat it like a glowing bar of plutonium, pick up with long-handled pincers, put it in a lead box, and take it to your spiritual father or mother for assessment. If a mistake is made either in accepting or rejecting it, the danger and responsibility attaches to the elder and not you.

If this spiritual visitation makes you feel excited, it's not from God. If it makes you feel superior to others, its base character should be obvious.

Q: *WHAT KIND OF "PEACE" DOES THE JESUS PRAYER AIM AT? DOES IT MEAN MAKING YOUR MIND EMPTY?*

No. When I think of "empty," I think of Jesus' story of a man who had been freed from a demon, but who hadn't claimed that interior space for God. The demon returns to his former "house" and finds it "empty, swept, and put in order" (Mt. 12:43–45). This story is not easy to understand, but it doesn't make emptiness sound like a good thing.

The silence that is the goal of the Jesus Prayer is not an empty silence. It is a listening silence. If you were in a noisy place and someone asked you an important question, you'd try to find a quiet place where you could focus on it, where you could *think*. That's the kind of silence we're after. It is a listening silence, expectant, rather than mental vacancy.

In a way, silence is the opposite of what we expect. Doesn't it seem like the presence of God would be, if nothing else, noisy? That it would bowl you over? Remember Elijah, who stood on the mountain before the Lord. "And behold, the LORD passed by, and a great and strong wind rent the mountains, and broke in pieces the rocks before the LORD, but the LORD was not in the wind; and after the wind an earthquake, but the LORD was not in the earthquake; and after the earthquake a fire, but the LORD was not in the fire; and after the fire a still small voice" (1 Kings 19:11–12).

That "still small voice" is more like what we're looking for. So don't expect something overwhelming and showy, but instead something subtle but real. Silence is necessary because we're trying to learn *how* to hear something; we must learn discernment, in order to be safe in a realm of deceptive spiritual powers. My son Steve is a piano tuner in his spare time, and even though electronic tuners are a big help in that business, there is no replacement for acquiring an exquisite sense of pitch. If you picture yourself trying to gain that ability, to be able to tell C from C# while it's hanging in the air, then you know the kind of silence I mean. (Steve tells me many homeowners try to make polite conversation while he's tuning their piano. Please don't.) So this is not an empty or passive silence, but one that marshals all your attention as you listen closely, carefully.

The Jesus Prayer is part of the *hesychast* tradition, a word that means the silence borne of awe. "Be still, and know that I am God" (Ps. 46:10). "For thus said the Lord GOD, the Holy One of Israel, 'In returning and rest you shall be saved; in quietness and in trust shall be your strength'" (Isa. 30:15).

Q: CAN I SAY THE JESUS PRAYER AS AN INTERCESSION, PUTTING SOMEONE ELSE'S NAME INSTEAD OF "ME"?

Yes, and I expect people do that naturally all the time. It wouldn't fall under the umbrella of the discipline of the Jesus Prayer, which has the goal of quieting and simplifying the mind and focusing it solely on Christ, but there's certainly no reason not to use some of your intercessory prayer time in this way.

So you could insert the name of someone you're praying for into the Jesus Prayer, or simply pray "have mercy on us," standing beside the person in need. Someone recently recommended to me a prayer for a strained relationship: "Lord Jesus Christ, bless Linda, and rescue me by her prayers." In your battle against pride and habitual sin, acknowledge your need for the prayers even of the difficult people in your life. It's strong medicine.

I find personally that if I start out praying, "Have mercy on Tom," I tend to switch back to, "Have mercy on me," without noticing, as I get further into the Prayer. I think this is because of the unity I begin to feel with Tom as I pray—both Tom and I under the great heartbeat of the universe.

Elder Porphyrios (AD 1906–91), a contemporary Greek elder who was a hospital chaplain during World War II, wrote to one of his spiritual children,

> When we pray for others we say, "Lord Jesus Christ, have mercy on me," and not "have mercy on him." In this way we make them one with ourselves. Prayer for others that is made gently and with deep love is selfless and has great benefit. It brings grace to the person who prays and also to the person for whom he is praying. When you have great love and this love moves you to prayer, then the waves of love are transmitted and affect the person for whom you are praying and you create around him a shield of protection and you influence him, you lead him toward what is good. When he sees your efforts, God bestows his grace abundantly on both you and on the person you are praying for. But we must die to ourselves. Do you understand?

I recently heard someone say, "My favorite kind of prayer is worry." I know what that's like. I spend enough time in what I call "handwringing" prayer, basically saying to God, "Do something! Do something!" I can tell that this is not authentic prayer, because it's not a conversation. I'm talking, not listening. Elder Porphyrios shows a different way of going about it, and though I'm not very good at it yet, I can catch a glimmer of what he means.

Q: *CAN I SAY THE JESUS PRAYER DURING CHURCH?*

There is a long tradition of using the Jesus Prayer in place of services, if you can't get to church. For example, a monk may be told to say six hundred repetitions for the Midnight Office, six hundred for Vespers, and so on.

Using the Prayer while attending services is a different question. Some say that it is all right to do this if the hymns and prayers are overly familiar, and you are having trouble keeping your mind on them. Others say, no, that you should always be praying along with the community. It's possible to do both at the same time, I think; if part of my brain is filled up with the Jesus Prayer, the leftover part is paying attention to the prayers of the service, instead of just roaming free. It's common to see monastics and clergy standing in worship with their prayer ropes passing through their fingers.

Q: *COULD YOU PRAY THE JESUS PRAYER ALONG WITH OTHER PEOPLE, EITHER SILENTLY OR OUT LOUD?*

At the Monastery of St. John the Baptist in Essex, England, the community gathers to offer the Jesus Prayer in place of the morning and evening services. From 7:00 to 9:00 AM, and from 5:00 to 7:00 PM, the nuns, monks, and visitors gather in the darkened church. A single voice in the congregation begins repeating the Jesus Prayer, clearly, reverently, in one of any number of languages. After one hundred repetitions, another voice takes up the Prayer in another language. This is a profoundly affecting experience, and I hope you get a chance to visit one day. But this practice is not widespread, and may even be unique to this monastery.

Apart from that, I don't know of another case of communal use of the Prayer, but a recent book describes the experience of two Anglicans who met to say the Prayer together for many years. Brother Ramon, a Franciscan monk, and Simon Barrington-Ward, retired Bishop of Coventry, found their long-standing friendship enhanced by this practice, and their book, *Praying the Jesus Prayer Together*, was published in the United States in 2004.

Q: *IT SOUNDS LIKE THE JESUS PRAYER IS ALL ABOUT HAVING SPIRITUAL EXPERIENCES, WHICH, NO MATTER HOW ELEVATED, HAVE NO IMPACT ON THE WORLD.*

On the contrary, the Prayer lifts you into the heart of God, where you see all of Creation through his eyes. It's hard for us to maintain that holistic sense these days. Christians get plenty of contempt from the world, which cannot see value in the spiritual aspects of our faith, and commends only the things we do that benefit the world. So we absorb the idea that prayer is pointless and self-centered, and only social action is worthwhile. There is not much sense any more that the two might go together, and that helping the poor could be an expression of the flow of prayer within you.

The Jesus Prayer can help put it back together again, so that your service to the world is linked once again to real, individual human beings. You become able to perceive suffering in all its guises, seeing that even those whose lives look enviable can still be shattered by emotional pain or physical disease. (Think of how sad those celebrities must be, whose genuine heartbreak is fodder for eager, gloating gossip.) The Jesus Prayer opens you to perceive the real sorrows in the lives of other human beings, and enhances your compassion. There is, in reality, no such thing as a "mass" of people; there are only individuals, each with his or her own relationship to God. With time you will get better at perceiving this, and praying in unity with God for the sorrows of the whole world.

As you shed the fatal impulse of self-defense ("Whoever would save his life will lose it," Mt. 16:25), as you die to self, your vision clears and you can better see the scope of God's work in the world. Then your intercessory prayer gets more in tune with God's will, and correspondingly more effective.

I picture something like a giant wagon wheel. Individual people are lined up all around the rim, and as one looks to another the distance seems so great. But if we go up our spoke to the hub, we find ourselves at the center, where everything comes together.

Prayer is like that. By bringing your mind into the presence of God, you stand at the center where he rules and sustains all. At that place, prayer really does change things.

Those who gain the higher reaches of the Prayer, the saints on earth, are known for the miracles wrought by their prayers, and for their God-given insight into people and situations they could not know by natural means. A great deal of their constant prayer is taken up with intercession for the world and its sorrows. Orthodox Christians believe that these prayers preserve the world, strengthen the remaining good wherever it lies, and fight alongside the powers of heaven against those that cherish cruelty and relish the suffering of the innocent.

"For we are not contending against flesh and blood, but against the principalities, against the powers, against the world rulers of this present darkness, against the spiritual hosts of wickedness in the heavenly places" (Eph. 6:12).

Elder Sophrony Sakharov (AD 1896–1993) described how a prayerful person makes a continual cycle, going from the presence of God to the sorrows of the world, which then send him back to the presence of God. "When, moved by great love, a man prays for the world, he reaches a state in which he is utterly unsparing of himself, and when this interior sacrifice is consummated, his soul accedes to a profound peace that comprehends all things. But once the prayer is over, seeing the world plunged in suffering and darkness, the soul is moved to pray again. And so it goes on, until life is terminated."

Q: DESPITE EVERYTHING, IT STILL DOESN'T SEEM LIKE GOD IS REALLY HERE. I DON'T KNOW IF IT REALLY IS POSSIBLE TO HAVE DIRECT CONTACT WITH GOD.

We easily say that God is always with us, but we often don't act that way; we act as if he's just kind of nearby. There's a companion thought going along with this, which has to do with God's love. We know that God is love. We teach this to our children, we sing about it, and when anyone asks about our faith we stress God's endless love. But we don't give evidence in our daily lives that we believe it. We say God loves us, but we behave as if we think God is *fond* of us.

These two half-beliefs link together. Think about it: if God truly is everywhere, he knows everything. He sees every second of our lives. He watches every action, he listens to every thought. He knows us *real* well. He knows the things we don't want anyone to know; he knows even the things we don't know, things we keep shoving down, away from awareness. God is in the very matrix of reality, at the boundary between energy and matter, and all Creation exists in him, because "in him all things hold together" (Col. 1:17). There is no moment, no fragment of a thought or an impulse that you have, that escapes his awareness.

Something I started noticing a few years ago was that there was a word that, if I said it in a speech, the audience would freeze. That word is *loneliness*. We are wracked with loneliness, I think, as a side effect of the consumerist quest for autonomy. Every manufacturer wants you to buy one for yourself and a separate one for your wife or child or roommate, because you buy more stuff that way. You demonstrate your originality and rebelliousness by buying the blue one instead of the green one. So we are insulated against each other, each trying to be a rebel and march to a different drummer. The highest virtue is niceness. We don't try for the really strenuous aspects of good character any more, such as loyalty or longsuffering—we just want to be nice, and to be left alone.

From that perspective, it feels as if God is watching us from about a block away, and when he looks our direction he gives us a generic smile. But if God really sees all the way through us, his presence is more immediate, and our relation to him more urgent, than we suppose. Earlier we considered this verse from the book of Revelation: "For you say, I am rich, I have prospered, and I need nothing; not knowing that you are wretched, pitiable, poor, blind, and naked" (Rev. 3:17). We don't even know that we are pitiable, yet still he has pity on us. And he, like the good Samaritan, does not allow us to founder in our lonely, nonconformist niceness. He is ready to take us up from our wretchedness and begin our healing.

If it is true that God knows us, and if it is also true that he nevertheless loves us, then his love is something we can scarcely conceive. It is like nothing we encounter on earth. As the book of Hebrews says, "Our God is a consuming fire" (Heb. 12:29).

The Jesus Prayer is designed to help you, day by day, turn your face into this blazing love of God. It helps us perceive that God is truly "everywhere present and filling all things" (as is said in the Orthodox prayer to the Holy Spirit); he is above and below and through us, and within every person we meet. It helps us realize that even though he knows us uncomfortably well, he loves us with a relentless, transforming love.

For the love of God *will* transform you. When the love of God is through with you, you will be shot through with his light. You will be changed into something you never expected to be. You will be what he planned you to be from the beginning—the only one of you in the universe.

Q: *I REALLY DON'T THINK I HAVE THE PERSONALITY FOR THIS; I DON'T THINK GOD CAN DO MUCH WITH ME.*

There's a story of the Desert Fathers concerning two monks who went to visit some of the luminaries of that age. First they went to see the famed ascetic Abba Arsenius. He had been a wealthy senator in Rome, and was known for his profound humility, sobriety, and penitence. (It is said that noble, silver-haired Arsenius was very handsome, except that he had wept for his sins so long that his eyelashes had washed away.) The two monks traveled a long way to get to his rustic cell, but once they had greeted the old man and sat down, silence reigned. The monks began to feel uneasy and took their leave.

Next they decided to see another giant of the desert, the former gang leader Abba Moses. This large, physically powerful man had been a robber and murderer before coming to Christ. "The Abba welcomed them joyfully and took leave of them with delight," a very different reception than they'd had from Arsenius.

When the monks returned and told about their journey, a fellow monk who heard the story was puzzled by the difference between the two holy men. "He prayed to God saying, 'Lord, explain this matter to me: for Thy name's sake the one flees from men, and the other, for Thy name's sake, receives them with open arms.'" This prayer was answered by a vision. "Then two large boats were shown to him on a river, and he saw Abba Arsenius and the Spirit of God sailing in one, in perfect peace; and in the other was Abba Moses with the angels of God, and they were all eating honey cakes."

So God can use any kind of personality, any kind of person; he only made one of you, and he has a plan for what you will be. The one light of Christ is like a flame shining out through millions of lanterns. But each lantern is made of different colored glass. You are the only person God made who is exactly like you; and if you fail to be filled with the light of Christ, you will eternally deprive the kingdom of God of one particular shade of radiance. The French philosopher Léon Bloy said: "There is only one tragedy: to fail to become a saint."

When you put together the force of God's love with the self you know yourself to be, the secret self that God already knows better than you do—when you put those two things together, then you will begin to know what it is to be free. You cannot grasp the love of God until you know how much you need it. Then you will know the truth—you will even know the truth about yourself—and the truth will set you free.

"And we all, with unveiled face, beholding the glory of the Lord, are being changed into his likeness from one degree of glory to another" (2 Cor. 3:18).

For Further Reading

Overview

Bajis, Jordan. *Common Ground: An Introduction to Eastern Orthodox Christianity for the American Christian.* Minneapolis: Light and Life Publishing, 1996.

Gillquist, Fr. Peter. *Becoming Orthodox: A Journey to the Ancient Christian Faith.* Ben Lomond, CA: Conciliar Press, 1992.

Hopko, Fr. Thomas. *The Orthodox Faith.* 4 vols. Brooklyn, OH: Orthodox Christian Publications Center, 1972.

Payton, James. *Light from the Christian East: An Introduction to the Orthodox Tradition.* Downers Grove, IL: Intervarsity Press, 2007.

Schmemann, Fr. Alexander. *The Historical Road of Eastern Orthodoxy.* Crestwood, NY: St. Vladimir's Seminary Press, 1977.

Ware, Bishop Kallistos. *The Orthodox Church.* London: Penguin Books, 1991.

The Jesus Prayer

Anonymous. *The Way of a Pilgrim* (many publishers).

Behr-Sigel, Elisabeth. *The Place of the Heart: An Introduction to Orthodox Spirituality.* Torrance, CA: Oakwood Publications, 1992.

Brianchaninov, St. Ignatius. *On the Prayer of Jesus.* Berwick, ME: Ibis Press, 2006.

Igumen Chariton of Valamo, ed. *The Art of Prayer*. Translated by E. Kadloubovsky and E.M. Palmer. Boston: Faber & Faber, 1981.

Gillet, Fr. Lev. "A Monk of the Eastern Church." *The Jesus Prayer*. Crestwood, NY: St. Vladimir's Seminary Press, 1987.

Golynsky-Mihailovsky, Abp. Anthony. *Two Elders on the Jesus Prayer*. Edited and compiled by N.M. Novikov. Translated by Igor V. Ksenzov. Hayesville, OH: Skete of the Entrance of the Theotokos into the Temple, 2008.

Hausherr, Irénée. *The Name of Jesus*. Kalamazoo, MI: Cistercian Publications, 1978.

Eastern Christian Spirituality & Asceticism

Bloom, Metropolitan Anthony. *Beginning to Pray*. New York: Paulist Press, 1970.

Braga, Fr. Roman. *Exploring the Inner Universe: Joy, the Mystery of Life*. Rives Junction, MI: Holy Dormition Monastery Press, 1996.

Brianchaninov, St. Ignatius. *The Arena*. Jordanville, NY: Holy Trinity Monastery, 1997.

Calciu, Fr. George. *Christ is Calling You! A Course in Catacomb Pastorship*. Forestville, CA: St. Herman of Alaska Brotherhood, 1998.

Colliander, Tito. *Way of the Ascetics: The Ancient Tradition of Discipline and Inner Growth*. Crestwood, NY: St. Vladimir's Seminary Press, 1985.

Evdokimov, Paul. *Ages of the Spiritual Life*. Crestwood, NY: St. Vladimir's Seminary Press, 1998.

Grisbrooke, W. Jardine, ed. *Spiritual Counsels of St. John of Kronstadt*. Crestwood, NY: St. Vladimir's Seminary Press, 1989.

Hausherr, Irénée. *Penthos: The Doctrine of Compunction in the Christian East*. Kalamazoo, MI: Cistercian Publications, 1982.

Hopko, Fr. Thomas. *The Lenten Spring: Readings for Great Lent*. Crestwood, NY: St. Vladimir's Seminary Press, 1983.

Logothetis, Archimandrite Spyridon. *The Heart: An Orthodox Christian Spiritual Guide*. Nafpakos, Greece: Holy Transfiguration Monastery, 2001.

Markides, Kyriacos. *The Mountain of Silence: A Search for Orthodox Spirituality*. New York: Doubleday, 2001.

Mathewes-Green, Frederica. *The Illumined Heart: The Ancient Christian Path of Transformation*. Brewster, MA: Paraclete Press, 2001.

Schmemann, Fr. Alexander. *For the Life of the World: Sacraments and Orthodoxy*. Crestwood, NY: St. Vladimir's Seminary Press, 1997.

Vlachos, Archimandrite Hierotheos. *The Illness and Cure of the Soul in the Orthodox Church*. Levadia, Greece: Holy Monastery of the Birth of the Theotokos, 2005.

———. *A Night in the Desert of the Holy Mountain: Discussion with a Hermit on the Jesus Prayer*. Levadia, Greece: Holy Monastery of the Birth of the Theotokos, 2003.

Ware, Bishop Kallistos. *The Orthodox Way*. Crestwood, NY: St. Vladimir's Seminary Press, 1995.

Classics

St. Athanasius. *On the Incarnation*. Crestwood, NY: St. Vladimir's Seminary Press, 1996.

The Desert Fathers: Sayings of the Early Christian Monks. Edited by Benedicta Ward. New York: Penguin Classics, 2003.

St. Isaac of Syria [or "of Nineveh"]. *On Ascetical Life*. Crestwood, NY: St. Vladimir's Seminary Press, 1989.

St. John Cassian. *The Conferences* (many translations).

St. John Chrysostom. *On Marriage and Family Life*. Crestwood, NY: St. Vladimir's Seminary Press, 1986.

St. John Climacus. *The Ladder of Divine Ascent*. Boston: Holy Transfiguration Monastery, 1978.

St. John of Damascus. *An Exact Exposition of the Orthodox Faith*.

The Philokalia. 4 vols. Translated by G.E.H. Palmer, Philip Sherrard, and Kallistos Ware. London and Boston: Faber and Faber, 1979–95.

Writings from the Philokalia on Prayer of the Heart. Translated by E. Kadloubovsky and G.E.H. Palmer. Boston: Faber & Faber, 1992.

Iconography, Hymnography, and Practice

Andreopoulos, Andreas. *The Sign of the Cross: The Gesture, the Mystery, the History*. Brewster, MA: Paraclete Press, 2006.

Forest, Jim. *Praying with Icons*. Maryknoll, NY: Orbis Books, 2008.

Lash, Archimandrite Ephrem, trans. *On the Life of Christ— Kontakia: Chanted Sermons by the Great Sixth-Century Poet and Singer*. San Francisco: HarperCollins, 1995.

Martin, Linette. *Sacred Doorways: A Beginner's Guide to Icons*. Brewster, MA: Paraclete Press, 2002.

Mathewes-Green, Frederica. *First Fruits of Prayer: A Forty-Day Journey through the Canon of St. Andrew*. Brewster, MA: Paraclete Press, 2006.

———. *The Lost Gospel of Mary: The Mother of Jesus in Three Ancient Texts*. Brewster, MA: Paraclete Press, 2007.

———. *The Open Door: Entering the Sanctuary of Icons and Prayer*. Brewster, MA: Paraclete Press, 2003.

Schork, R.J. *Sacred Song from the Byzantine Pulpit: Romanos the Melodist*. Gainesville, FL: University Press of Florida, 1995.

Williams, Benjamin D., and H. Anstall. *Orthodox Worship: A Living Continuity with the Temple, the Synagogue, and the Early Church*. Minneapolis: Light and Life Publishing, 1990.

Bible & Bible Commentary

The Orthodox Study Bible. Lomond, CA: Conciliar Press, 2008. (Includes an English translation of the Greek Septuagint Old Testament and the New Testament, with commentary based on the church fathers.)

St. John Chrysostom (347–407), was surnamed "Golden Mouth" for his eloquence, and his bible commentaries and sermons are highly valued. He is only one of many brilliant Church Fathers whose commentaries and other works are made available on the Internet through the Christian Classics Ethereal Library. The comprehensive 37-volume series that has been scanned in is also available from the CCEL on a disk, and in hardback from Hendrickson Publishers (Peabody, MA, 1994).

Biographies and Teachings of Saints

Balan, Archimandrite Ioanichie. *Shepherd of Souls: The Life and Teachings of Elder Cleopa.* Platina, CA: St. Herman of Alaska Brotherhood, 2000.

Bouteneff, Vera. *Father Arseny, 1873–1973: Priest, Prisoner, Spiritual Father.* Crestwood, NY: St. Vladimir's Seminary Press, 1998.

———. *Father Arseny: A Cloud of Witnesses.* Crestwood, NY: St. Vladimir's Seminary Press, 2001.

Gavrilia, Nun. *Mother Gavrilia: The Ascetic of Love.* Athens: Tertios, 1999.

Elder Porphyrios. *Wounded by Love: The Life and the Wisdom of Elder Porphyrios*. Edited by Sisters of the Holy Convent of Chrysopigi. Limni, Evia, Greece: Denise Harvey Publisher, 2005.

Sakharov, Archimandrite Sophrony. *Saint Silouan the Athonite*. Essex, UK: Patriarchal Stavropegic Monastery of St. John the Baptist, 1991.

————. *We Shall See Him as He Is*. Platina, CA: St. Herman of Alaska Brotherhood, 2006.

Velimirovic, St. Nikolai. *The Prologue of Ohrid: Lives of Saints, Hymns, Reflections, and Homilies for Every Day of the Year*. Alhambra, CA: Serbian Orthodox Diocese of Western America, 2002.

Contemporary Life in Orthodoxy

Cairns, Scott. *A Short Trip to the Edge: Where Earth Meets Heaven, A Pilgrimage*. San Francisco: HarperCollins, 2007.

Mathewes-Green, Frederica. *At the Corner of East and Now: A Modern Life in Ancient Christian Orthodoxy*. Ben Lomond, CA: Conciliar Press, 2009.

————. *Facing East: A Pilgrim's Journey into the Mysteries of Orthodoxy*. San Francisco: HarperSanFrancisco, 1997.

Notes

Part 1, Chapter 2

20   *two sides of the same coin*   Metropolitan Kallistos Ware, *The Orthodox Church* (London: Penguin Books, 1991), 10.

28   *which characterizes the Eastern Church*   Rt. Rev. Anthony Bloom, *Asceticism: Somatopsychic Techniques in Greek Orthodox Christianity*, Guild Lecture 95, (London: The Guild of Pastoral Psychology, 1957), 29–30.

29   *fanatical and does harm*   Sisters of the Holy Convent of Chrysopigi, ed. *Wounded by Love: The Life and Wisdom of Elder Porphyrios*, trans. John Raffan (Limni, Evia, Greece: Denise Harvey Publisher, 2005), 124–25.

Part 1, Chapter 3

41   *with Jesus as the compass*   Andreas Andreopoulos, *The Sign of the Cross* (Brewster, MA: Paraclete Press, 2006), 61.

Part 2, Questions and Answers

50   *should be pleasant to God*   Richard Wurmbrand, "With My Own Eyes," http://ancientfaith.com/files/uploads/wurmbrand_again.doc, 5.

52   *get used to moderation gradually*   Abp. Anthony Golynsky-Mihailovsky, *Two Elders on the Jesus Prayer*, ed. and comp. N.M. Novikov, trans. Igor V. Ksenzov

(Hayesville, OH: Skete of the Entrance of the Theotokos into the Temple, 2008), 51.

58 *in spirit and truth* W. Jardine Grisbrooke, ed., *Spiritual Counsels of St. John of Kronstadt* (Crestwood, NY: St. Vladimir's Seminary Press, 1989), 29–30.

75 *as you stand* St. John Cassian, *Conferences*, book X, chapter 10.

77 *by the name "Jesus" alone* Irénée Hausherr, *The Name of Jesus* (Kalamazoo, MI: Cistercian Publications, 1978), 63ff.

83 *read, watch, or examine something* Igumen Chariton of Valamo, ed., *The Art of Prayer*, trans. E. Kadloubovsky and E.M. Palmer (Boston: Faber and Faber, 1981), 83.

83 *the Prayer is dry food* Chariton, *Art of Prayer*, 98–99.

85 *fills the whole Creation* Grisbrooke, *Spiritual Counsels of St. John of Kronstadt*, 28.

86 *in our spiritual life* Chariton, *Art of Prayer*, 123.

88 *walking always in his presence* Chariton, *Art of Prayer*, 128.

94 *feel the activity of the Spirit directly* Metropolitan Kallistos Ware, "The Power of the Name," in Elisabeth Behr-Sigel, *The Place of the Heart* (Torrance, CA: Oakwood Publications, 1992), 138.

97 *all things are there* Pseudo-Macarius: *The Fifty Spiritual Homilies and the Great Letter*, ed. George Maloney (New York: Paulist Press), xvi. This author is called "Pseudo-Macarius" because scholarly opinion is that the author of these works is not the fourth-century Desert Father, but a fifth-century Syrian writer

who wrote in his name, to honor him (kind of like a "tribute band"). This is not uncommon; scholars assume that the works attributed to Dionysius the Areopagite (mentioned in Acts 17:34) were written by someone in the late fifth century, and the Letters of St. Anthony are thought to have come from the pen of a more educated writer. But these things move in waves, and now some are urging reconsideration of the possibility that Abba Macarius did write these works, and that St. Anthony was fully capable of composing such letters. I was recently invited to join a Facebook group called "People who refuse to prefix 'Pseudo' to Dionysius the Areopagite." This may not be a large group, but it sounds spunky.

102 *pattern described by Metropolitan Anthony Bloom* Bloom, *Asceticism*, 12–14.

104 *image of Our Lord Jesus Christ* Ibid., 14–17.

106 *the story was about him* N.M. Novikov, in his Introduction to Golynsky-Mihailovsky, *Two Elders on the Jesus Prayer*, 12.

106–13 *there were many doers who knew it by experience . . . years or decades* Golynsky-Mihailovsky, *Two Elders on the Jesus Prayer*, 34–72.

116 *and remain there* Bloom, *Asceticism*, 17.

116 *a bad prayer* Behr-Sigel, *The Place of the Heart*, 128.

116 *relaxation therapy* Ibid., 127.

121 *mental alienation and physiological disorders* Bloom, *Asceticism*, 18–19.

122 *anyone can achieve it* Chariton, *Art of Prayer*, 126.

123 *cannot arrive at it whenever we want to*   Ibid., 81.

123 *established in the heart*   Ibid., 127.

123 *attained by some mystics*   Ibid., 160.

128 *as separate individuals*   David Biello, "Searching for God in the Brain," *Scientific American Mind*, October 2007, http://www.sciam.com/article.cfm?id= searching-for-god-in-the-brain.

131 *and strengthen it there*   *Writings from the Philokalia on Prayer of the Heart*, trans. E. Kadloubovsky and G.E.H. Palmer (London and Boston: Faber and Faber, 1992), 33.

132 *an idol—'I'*   Chariton, *Art of Prayer*, 147.

134 *no myth is filled with such life*   "Einstein and Faith," *Time*, April 5, 2007, http://www.time.com/time/ magazine/article/0,9171,1607298-2,00.html.

137 *most authentic monk*   "Silouan the Athonite," Wikipedia, http://en.wikipedia.org/wiki/Silouan_the_Athonite.

138 *prayer for the whole world*   Archimandrite Sophrony Sakharov, *Saint Silouan the Athonite* (Essex, UK: Patriarchal Stavropegic Monastery of St. John the Baptist, 1991), 162–63.

138 *that he has shot an enemy*   Dan Baum, "The Price of Valor," *The New Yorker*, July 12 & 19, 2004, 44–52.

139 *succumbed to hallucinations*   Rachel MacNair, *Perpetration-Induced Traumatic Stress* (Westport, CT: Praeger, 2002), 46–48.

140 *in the heart of a Communist murderer*   Wurmbrand, "With My Own Eyes," 6.

143   *be glory and praise forever*   St. Nikolai Velimirovic, *The Prologue of Ohrid* (Alhambra, CA: Serbian Orthodox Diocese of Western America, 2002), 1:650.

148   *understand what this means*   Grisbrooke, *Spiritual Counsels of St. John of Kronstadt*, 55.

150   *not responsible for these logismoi*   Kyriacos Markides, *Mountain of Silence* (New York: Doubleday, 2001), 124.

154   *gods in our own image*   Fr. Michael Shanbour, "Kids that Love Church: Orthodox Youth Ministry and Christian Education" (unpublished).

154   *the same thing as actually eating it?*   Markides, *Mountain of Silence*, 128.

159   *Do you understand?*   Sisters of the Holy Convent of Chrysopigi, *Wounded by Love*, 132.

164   *until life is terminated*   Sakharov, *Saint Silouan the Athonite*, 241.

167   *eating honey cakes*   Ward, *The Sayings of the Desert Fathers*, xxiv–xxv

About Paraclete Press

Who We Are

Paraclete Press is a publisher of books, recordings, and DVDs on Christian spirituality. Our publishing represents a full expression of Christian belief and practice—from Catholic to Evangelical, from Protestant to Orthodox.

We are the publishing arm of the Community of Jesus, an ecumenical monastic community in the Benedictine tradition. As such, we are uniquely positioned in the marketplace without connection to a large corporation and with informal relationships to many branches and denominations of faith.

What We Are Doing

BOOKS—Paraclete publishes books that show the richness and depth of what it means to be Christian. Although Benedictine spirituality is at the heart of all that we do, we publish books that reflect the Christian experience across many cultures, time periods, and houses of worship. We publish books that nourish the vibrant life of the church and its people— books about spiritual practice, formation, history, ideas, and customs.

We have several different series, including the best-selling Living Library, Paraclete Essentials, and Paraclete Giants series of classic texts in contemporary English; A Voice from the Monastery—men and women monastics writing about living a spiritual life today; award-winning literary faith fiction and poetry; and the Active Prayer Series that brings creativity and liveliness to any life of prayer.

RECORDINGS—From Gregorian chant to contemporary American choral works, our music recordings celebrate sacred choral music through the centuries. Paraclete distributes the recordings of the internationally acclaimed choir Gloriæ Dei Cantores, praised for their "rapt and fathomless spiritual intensity" by American Record Guide, and the Gloriæ Dei Cantores Schola, which specializes in the study and performance of Gregorian chant. Paraclete is also the exclusive North American distributor of the recordings of the Monastic Choir of St. Peter's Abbey in Solesmes, France, long considered to be a leading authority on Gregorian chant.

DVDs—Our DVDs offer spiritual help, healing, and biblical guidance for life issues: grief and loss, marriage, forgiveness, anger management, facing death, and spiritual formation.

Learn more about us at our Web site:
www.paracletepress.com, or call us toll-free at 1-800-451-5006.

Also by Frederica Mathewes-Green

ISBN: 978-1-55725-611-9
234 pp., $14.95

First Fruits of Prayer

First Fruits of Prayer brings to life the prayer experience of first-millennium Christianity through immersion in this poetic hymn, a beautiful work that is still chanted by Christians around the world each Lent. It weaves together Old and New Testament Scriptures with prayers of hope and repentance and offers ancient ways of seeing Christ that still feel new today.

ISBN: 978-1-55725-574-7
166 pp., $14.95

The Open Door

Encounter twelve of the world's most significant Orthodox icons with one of today's best-loved spiritual writers as your guide.

"*The Open Door* provides an open window into a radically different approach to spiritual formation, one that is more ancient/Eastern than modern/Western, one that feels refreshingly new as well as seasoned, rich, and time-tested."

—Brian McLaren, author of *A Generous Orthodoxy*

Available from most booksellers or through Paraclete Press: www.paracletepress.com; 1-800-451-5006.
Try your local bookstore first.

Also by Frederica Mathewes-Green

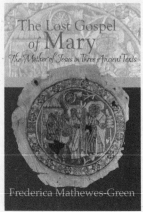

ISBN: 978-1-55725-536-5
159 pp., $19.95

The Lost Gospel of Mary

How did the first Christians view Mary? How did the mother of Jesus become the Theotokos? Mathewes-Green opens up the Virgin Mary's early life, offering a window into her centrality to the Christian faith in new and sometimes startling ways.

"When it comes to spending time with the mother of our Lord, this book is second only to Scripture."

—Lauren Winner, author of *Mudhouse Sabbath.*

ISBN: 978-1-55725-553-2
112 pp., $12.95

The Illumined Heart
Capture the Vibrant Faith of Ancient Christians

Drawing on Christian writings throughout the early centuries, Frederica illuminates the ancient, transcultural faith of the early church.

"Breathtakingly countercultural, and worth more to the honest seeker than shelves of what passes for practical spirituality these days."

—Rod Dreher, *The New York Post*

Available from most booksellers or through Paraclete Press:
www.paracletepress.com; 1-800-451-5006.
Try your local bookstore first.